Something i wrote myself

An Anthology
1981-82

Editor: Robert Fox, Writer in Residence
and Literature Coordinator
Designer: Micheal Milligan, Design Arts Coordinator
and Graphic Designer
Assistant Designer: Shawn Wolfe
Production Assistant: David Flaherty
Cover and Title Page Photographer: Will Shively

The Ohio Arts Council gratefully acknowledges the generosity and donation of service of George Skeele, Jr., Printers' Service, Columbus.

Published by the Ohio Designer Craftsmen
for the Ohio Arts Council

Printed in the United States of America

Library of Congress Cataloging in Publication Data
Main entry under title:

Something i wrote myself.

Poems from the Ohio Arts Council's Artists in Education Program.

1. School verse, American—Ohio. 2. American poetry—Ohio. 3. American poetry—20th century. I. Fox, Robert, 1943– . II. Ohio Arts Council.
PS591.S3S58 1983 811'54'0809282 83-12156
ISBN 0-913335-01-0

In Memorium:

Walt McCaslin
Reginald Brooks

One of the happiest outcomes of the Ohio Arts Council's efforts to bring an appreciation of the arts to constituents of all ages are our anthologies of children's poetry. This collection, like its predecessors, is the result of the exciting interaction of writers in our Artists in Education program with schoolchildren throughout the state. As you will see, creative writing for these young people is an experience filled with vitality.

A word of thanks is in order to Vonnie Sanford and Kay Allen, AIE coordinator and assistant coordinator respectively; Council members who have strongly encouraged our outreach efforts in the schools; Bob Fox, our writer in residence; and Micheal Milligan, the OAC's graphic designer and design arts coordinator. Without the enthusiasm and dedication of these professionals and our support staff, this delightful anthology would not have seen print.

Wayne P. Lawson, Ph.D.
Executive Director

Lucky you!

You have a copy of *Something i wrote myself* in your hands. It is, indeed, a remarkable book written by the children of Ohio—children from all the varied parts of the state: inner city, small town, suburban, rural, lake country and the southern hills. They represent a new generation of students who have discovered that they can create poems. And they have so much to say about a myriad of things. They speak of favorite colors, songs, sports, the universe, their families, familiar events of everyday life and deep emotions; the sort of feelings one might be too shy or inhibited to share. The children have learned that their feelings are similar to those of the great poets.

These poems, selected from many residencies, represent the work of the hundreds of new poets who discover themselves in Ohio schools. They celebrate themselves in the residency experience and they celebrate the poets and writers that guided the way. Poetry no longer belongs to the past in thick and tedious textbooks. It has become re-established as a living art form. This book is proof.

Find a quiet corner, read and enjoy.

Vonnie Sanford
Artists in Education Coordinator

INTRODUCTION

The dedications for this, our fourth statewide anthology begin things on a sombre note which should be explained. Walt McCaslin was arts reporter for the Dayton *Journal Herald*. He was a staunch supporter of the arts, supporter of the AIE program and of our previous anthologies. He was murdered by his teenage son who had gone berserk in their home in Yellow Springs. Reginald Brooks was a teenage boy attending Shaw High School in East Cleveland, who happened to be in an English class visited by poet Barbara Angell as part of a long-term residency. One night he was murdered by his father who had gone berserk.

Before his death Reggie had written a poem which Barbara Angell reprints in the introduction to her section, work from Shaw that year. It is a poem Reggie would not have written if it were not for the residency. But what makes it more interesting and meaningful for us is the unusual self-realization that Reggie expressed in the piece work. The medium of the poem, in one classroom period, enabled the boy to verbalize who he was in the brief span of his existence.

Living and dying miles apart, without the possibility of ever meeting one another, Walt and Reggie are suddenly tied together, not by the tragic ironies of their deaths as much as by poetry. Walt appreciated poetry as an art, and for its role in society. Reggie happened to be in a certain class on a certain day and turned out a memorable piece of writing.

The level of consciousness achieved in Reggie's poem is what we who work in and administer these kinds of programs hold as an ideal. It is an individual awakening of human potential, an awareness of beauty against the backdrop of the vulnerability and brevity of life itself. This is what art is, why we practice it as artists, or engage in its appreciation. All forms of art give us meaning, what used to be called "truth" in an otherwise chaotic and often random-seeming existence. Art deals in multitudes of truths and meanings, not in simple abolutes.

Contemporary physicists no longer describe physical reality in terms of absolutes but rather as a multitude of possibilities. The absolute nature of reality which scientists had taken for granted for centuries has been replaced by a new view in the study of quantum mechanics, which examines reality at its most fundamental level, studies the nature and behavior of atomic particles. Newton's laws often do not work on the atomic level. There are no laws or absolutes on this level except those that predict and deal with uncertainty. We learn from physicists that there are many possible realities (truths), and that the presence of an observer immediately influences the behavior of what is being observed.*

The multiplicity of today's art scene confuses those who profess knowledge and control over their respective genres. A revolution has been occurring in all the arts in this country for better than 20 years. Quality writing and publishing, quality dance, theatre, painting and sculpture occur in sparsely populated regions and small towns as well as in big cities. While the east and west coasts still host the largest numbers of practicing artists, they no longer exert as strong as influence over what is being created and enjoyed.

Mass media publications however, barely and reluctantly acknowledge the existence of widespread and high quality arts activity. One would not know that there was a revolution in the arts by reading the New York *Times* or watching the major TV networks. But the activity itself is what is important: it means that art is accessible and that it has meaning for anyone who cares or chances to get involved in it.

Often in the AIE program resident artists uncover brilliance in unexpected places—in those students labelled as "problem students" or as "Educably Mentally Retarded." Students who are not encouraged to find ways of expressing themselves will respond with disruptive behavior or will shut themselves off. A number of poems in this and previous anthologies have come from children labelled in either of the two categories. Fortunately, our public educational establishment, which has generally not had the time or money for art as "frill" has recently begun to understand and acknowledge the importance of the arts as a basic in a sound educational program.

For the reader who has gone through school acquiring a bad taste for poetry, I offer the following sonnet to sweeten your taste. It emerged too late to include in the previous collection. The introduction is by Devon McNamara, who was the resident poet.

This sonnet was made out loud, on the last day of my residency, in a senior English class, and the girl who took the lead and made it her poem, had, I believe, lately emerged from a "reform facility."

THE WAYS SONNETS WORK ON A CRUMMY DAY

I think I will go home today and sleep
My mind rolls off into a weary dream
Through pools of water, clouded, bland, and deep
Till shadows, walking, aren't what they seem...

Children gather falling stars from trees
They hoist the sun from his mysterious rest
They taunt the moon, blow bubbles in the seas
They fold the school and toss it in the clouds
They spin it wildly into sheets of rain
Till lollipops emerge and dance in crowds
And sweeten the rainbowed air again. Again!
This bright shower is all my poem.
Sign it. Sing it. Sail it home.

—Sherrie Browning
mostly, with a little
help from her friends
North Gallia High School
Linda Rusk, Teacher

As in previous anthologies, the students' work is not offered as polished writing, but as astonishingly good first takes—astonishing, because of the way students intuitively express themselves in language, given the opportunity. To quote Walt McCaslin, writing of our first anthology, "This *is* poetry, and we need it."

—Robert Fox
Writer in Residence

*The truths of the new physics are a form of poetry in themselves which parallel the ancient teachings of Zen Buddhism. Gary Zukav makes these parallels in his book, *The Dancing WuLi Masters,* available in a popular paper edition.

HOW TO USE THIS ANTHOLOGY
and SOME ADDITIONAL RESOURCES

This collection can be used in conjunction with the Artists in Education *Directory* but shouldn't be used in place of it. Be sure to have a current *Directory* when selecting writers, and be sure to have a copy of the short-term guidelines as well—they are no longer published as part of this anthology. For those and other bits of information about the Artists in Education Program, write to:

Vonnie Sanford, Coordinator
Artists in Education Program
Ohio Arts Council
727 East Main Street
Columbus, OH 43205

As in the past, the anthology is organized alphabetically by the last name of the resident writer. Check the table of contents for the writers name.

Where available, we included a picture of the writer and a sample of his or her work. Some of the writers included here are no longer in the program and we were unable to contact them.

In our 1978 collection, *Good Old Poems/I Love Them,* we included poems by teachers who participated in the program. That proved to be a popular feature and we include it again this year.

Teachers often find our anthologies a useful resource in presenting creative writing in the classroom and constantly ask for additional resources that can be used once the residency is concluded. Rather than present an extensive bibliography here, I'd like to refer the interested teacher and writer primarily to Teachers & Writers Collaborative, 84 Fifth Avenue, New York, NY 10011. In addition to publishing many fine resource books, such as Parts I and II of *The Whole Word Catalog,* and *The Poetry Connection,* T & W also distributes books by such innovative writers as Kenneth Koch and Herbert Kohl, published by other presses. T & W also publishes a bimonthly magazine with up-to-date articles by writers and teachers, and reviews of new books.

Some additional recommended offerings are:

Teaching Language Arts Creatively, by Mimi Brodsky Chenfeld, Harcourt Brace Jovanovich, 1978. "It is obvious from everything about this book that Ms. Chenfeld cares about children. But, she also cares about teachers. This book is inspiring and useful. It is an excellent addition to any teacher's bookshelf." (From a review by Karen Pool in ALTERNATIVE.) Forthcoming in 1983 by Ms. Chenfeld, also from Harcourt, is *Creative Activities For Young Children.*

The Power of Creative Writing: A Handbook of Insights, Activities, and Information to Get Your Students Involved, by Bernard Percy, Prentice-Hall, 1981. In reviewing the book in *T & W Magazine,* Susan Mernit writes: "Percy has a clear idea of the dynamics that go into structuring a creative writing program, prior to beginning to write, so that children will experience success and appreciation rather than anxiety and failure...His suggestion on making the classroom into a safe, secure, learning environment could educate any teacher."

Two other statewide anthologies of note come from:

The Montana Arts Council
1280 South Third St. West
Missoula, MT 59801

and

California Poets in the Schools
San Francisco State University
Humanities Office
1600 Holloway Avenue
San Francisco, CA 94132

TABLE OF CONTENTS

BARBARA ANGELL
2841 Edgehill
Cleveland, OH 44118
(216) 371-0441

Elem and Sec

Barbara began as a visual artist and illustrator and started writing poetry when her children were young, as she needed to keep her paints and brushes out of reach of small fingers. Her poems have been widely published in literary magazines and anthologies, and a collection of her work, *Games and Puzzles,* was published by Cleveland State University Press in 1978. She has been a member of a women's performing poetry troupe and sits on the literature advisory panel of the OAC. She has taught poetry in elementary and high schools in Beachwood, Shaker, Cleveland Heights, and Grafton in Lorain County. During the school years: 1981-82, and 1982-83 she conducted a long-term residency at Shaw High School in East Cleveland, a residency coordinated by University Circle, Inc. and supported in part by grants from the Gund and Martha Holden Jennings foundations in addition to the OAC.

WHAT IS

Awake,
startled by 4 a.m.
in the middle of September,
the moon's eyes
in my face,

I go out into the yard,
watch the leaves quivering
a few stars, the dipper, Orion,
the luminous rim of night,

awake with that murmur,
your life is going, your life
is going, nothing you've done
is what you meant to do.

Yet the trees breathing
and the shining silence
say: this is here,
this is what is,
listen.

—b angell

THE POETS AND THE POEMS

Probably the best known poems at Shaw High School is one written not by a famous poet, or even by a poet at all, but by a student who probably never intended to write a poem. Reggie Brooks was in Carol Blaha's Vocational English class when I went in once a week for six weeks to introduce the students to poetry writing. They had no choice. Evervone in the class wrote. Some liked it, some fidgeted, some were bored, some were intrigued.

I told the students that poetry is a picture in words, a picture of a piece of time or experience, some memory or image that stands out in your mind. And as we perceive everything we know about the world through our senses, we recall our sense impressions when we recreate that image in words. The right choice of words can make that piece of time come alive again. In my first class visit I asked students to write a sense impression of some incident in their lives or some scene which they see in their mind's eye. I asked them to place themselves there and write as if they are looking out.

Later I asked them to write a piece called "I Remember," and to recreate a time in their lives. In some classes I asked students to write their own personal definitions of words or things; to write as if they are noticing something for the first time. Poetry is not rhyming words, poetry is vision. Poets see and describe ordinary things in a new way. What is extraordinary about the ordinary?

I usually typed and copied works by published poets as examples which I read and discussed before the students wrote their own poems. One example I used "The Delight Song of Tsoai-Talee," in which contemporary American Indian poet, N. Scott Momaday, begins each line with "I am," describing himself in terms of the things in the world around him. Many of the "I Am" poems in this collection are based on that poem. Reggie Brooks wrote the following:

I AM

—Reginald Brooks

I am a vision
I am known
I am unknown
I am growing
I am developing
I am becoming smarter
I am learning of life
I am lucky for this time
I am watching and looking for the next time
I am glad I had a time
I am gone forever after this

I typed it up along with other students' work in a photocopied booklet.

On March 6, 1982 he was murdered by his father. After his death his poem circulated through school and was printed in the East Cleveland *Citizen*. The poem presents a great deal of self-awareness and an appreciation of the precariousness of life. Reggie left something which people could read and say, "Yes, that was something that Reggie knew, and something that we can know too."

One reason why I like to go into classrooms and press-gang students into writing poems is that a poem can be a small piece of yourself at a given moment. You have to search within yourself and bring something out. You have to imagine, remember, compare one thing to another. You have to use your powers of observation and invention. Many times the students would rather not.

At the end of a series of meetings I sometimes said to them, "Well, I know that lots of times when I came in you couldn't think of something and you weren't in the mood to write, but if I hadn't made you, you wouldn't have written a poem at all. Take a look on the typewritten page and tell me if your poem doesn't look better to you in print than when you wrote it down."

After I have been in a class for five or six time I collect everything the students have written. Often I type up the poems I like best; I like to, if I can, type one from each student. In each person's collection there is always a range. Some are better than others; some pieces work, some don't.

I like to work with entire classes, for the best and most surprising work often comes from students who would never have written a poem at all. When they have to invent, some students tap resources and images which surprise me and themselves as well.

—Barbara Angell

Shaw High School
East Cleveland

From Carol Blaha's Classes

DRACULA

He's a woman's fantasy
a man's nightmare
He's a woman's strength
a man's weakness
He's a woman's desire
a man's wonder
He's a woman's romance
a man's tragedy
He's a woman's bravery
a man's fear
He's a woman's spirit
a man's soul

—Dale Jones

SUMMER NIGHT

Dark, as to look into space
quiet and calm
breezy, like a night wind in autumn
slight music in a distance, like
a shopping mall radio while shopping
small sounds, crickets and the leaves of the trees
like the sounds of the sea in a sea shell
faint voices in a distance, that
come unexpectedly

—Dale Jones

I AM THE MAN OF YOUR DREAMS

I am the man of your dreams
I am loved and desired by many hungry women
I am sweet as a tangerine but very awesome
I am a white Arabian stallion rampaging the desert
I am superior over my fellow men
I am the lust of every woman's dream
I am the satisfier, companion, of any one's friend
I am the romance of a graceful night out
I am the champagne that you sip so slowly
I am a stubborn bull trampling his prey
I am love, in anyone's way
I am well put together, like a brand new car
    that would last a lifetime
I am the ultimate challenge in every way
I am the man of your dreams

—Artis Tucker

DAYDREAMS

In the middle of the afternoon
I am a prince, a golden groom,
A pirate on a desert isle,
A king of the River Nile.
All this and more I can be,
For my daydreams are dreams of me.

—Samuel Harris

ELBERON

Blossoming green trees to climb,
baseball and swimming,
girls and boys and girls,
hot lazy days under
beautiful blue,
running and playing
and a baby's restless cry.

—Samuel Harris

MY CAT, MY PET

A cat sneaking through the house
A skilled spy watching everyone
An acrobat doing flips under the big top
An assassin stalking his prey
A majestic king surveying his kingdom
A lowly peasant begging

—Samuel Harris

I AM TIME AND MOTION

I am time and motion
I am grace and beauty
I am infinity
I am music in time
I am a violin with rosined bow
I am poetic and joyful
I am a lisp of wind through a corridor
I am a canyon that echoes with every whisper
I am time and motion

—Samuel Harris

AN ELIZABETHAN MAN

Here I sit in my cold room,
And I am cast in dusty gloom,
When hearths and wine await somewhere
My spirits rise and take me there.

I leave my body to guard that place,
To dwell in anguish among the waste,
Whilst I fly high in my endless search
For love in life upon this earth.

I govern lands and command the seas,
Armadas kneel and armies flee.
Although against me the world may conspire,
I live for a candlelit dinner and you by the fire.

—Richard Trower

THE MANY PHASES OF BEING A WOMAN

1.

You see her as a child
with a never ending
chain of questions.

2.

You see her growing to
the heights of perfection

3.

She may seem
beautiful or ugly at the time
but it depends on her mood

4.

She blooms as a
caterpillar does

5.

She is a teenager
with her first love, and
then her first broken heart

6.

She is a cinderella
in a music box

7.
The glass of a gothic window

8.
The immovable stone
imbedded deep into the ground

9.
Heart made of
precious gems of the world,
then cold as ice

10.
Tender as a dove
flying peacefully, silently
over the ocean

11.
The many unexplainable
things she is that the world
may never know till time ends

12.
Mother, wife, worker, loner

13.
She goes on and on
but only she knows
when she ends

—Dawn Juanita Fowler

WHEN I AM FEELING SAD

When I am feeling sad
I think of the times I spent with my father,
how we would just go to the football and baseball games
and eat all the popcorn we could eat.

When I am feeling sad
I think of the times when my father showed me around
downtown,
busy streets, red lights, green lights, many people
in a rush.
Lines are very long at the games. Too much noise
A place where crime is a hobby. But I was safe.
I had my dad with me.

At night when we came home I saw
a man with a big hat in a big car.
He was hitting a lady with a short dress and wig.
I was scared, but
I had my dad with me.

—Vaughn Johnson

AN UNTITLED POEM

I'm an eagle in the air
I'm wild as wind
I'm a deer in the forest
I'm a steed without a rider
I'm a dog without a master
I'm a freed slave
I'm a child without parents
I am stone free

—John Dean

I AM

I am a door letting people in
I am a couch sinking in the floor
I am a toaster browning bread
I am a stove boiling water
I am a cupboard hiding goodies
I am a house protecting the inside from the outside

—Mistyne Johnson

WALKING IN A CLASS FOR THE FIRST TIME

Walking in a class for the first time
you wonder about people,
you hear yourself walking across the floor
listening to the muffled voices, wondering
if they're talking about you,
remembering the school you came from, and
then this one,
seeing the new people, leaving the others behind,
talking to the new teacher,
then sitting next to pretty girls,
smelling perfume.

To keep from being nervous, you take out a stick
of gum and taste the spearmint.
The sweet taste calms you down.
Hearing what the girls think about you,
a little bit,
seeing a room's color: sky blue with
the desks looking hand carved
by a master craftsman.

—Derrick Freeman

I IMAGINE HER

I imagine her as a golden bird,
A shadow against the noon sky.
I think of her on a dark night,
Replacing the moon shining high.

I remember her so very bright,
Deep in my heart I know not why.
Why do I imagine a golden bird,
I guess it replaces the noon sky.

—Bartholomew Cole

A CURE FOR SHYNESS

First you get a pocket full of money
a mask made to order of a famous movie star
an '82 Samborghini and a beautiful gir.
If you're still shy, at least you're rich.

—Charles Mays

REMEDY FOR A FUSSING MOTHER

5 whiskers from a quiet cat
3 sweet & sour candy hearts
a double of gin
a triple of brandy
a half quart of juice (any kind)

Mix all ingredients in a tall
quart size jar with a blender
until creamy. Serve in pint size
glass with two ice cubes.

Guaranteed to work within
15 min. of downing the hatch.

Present mixture in a thoughtful
manner.

—Bradley Thomas

CITY NIGHT

Stars bright
Darkness here
Slow moving traffic
        must get home

Lonely lady
    muggers out to get a cent
Streetlights
    glowing
        moths having fun
Everyone's asleep

—Hilary Hobson

BLACK NIGHT

I sit alone watching the
river boat fire's bright red
flames dance across the harbor

The shadow of a bird glides
across the cold black waves
of the lake

A new moon shines a golden
color across the waves

—Linda Provitt

BAMBOO LODGE

I sit alone inside a dark
bamboo grove

Play the song again

Long tunes the deep woods

people do not know

I go out and look at
the bright moon that shines
outside the dark
bamboo grove

—Linda Provitt

WHITE

The snow that falls from
the sky above
brings down little angels
telling us to be good,
so that we won't be seen
in white funeral homes
that bring such sorrow.

—Andrea Bell

BLACK

Sad
lonely
lost
failure
mysterious
magic

I am in a hidden cave

—Gilbert Abercrombie

I AM

I am what I am
I am Shawna
I am cool as a fan
I am smooth as a threat
I am as old as dead
I am as fooled as said
I am what I am

—Shawna Glaspy

THE TOUCH

The touch, soft, fragile.
A baby; very small,
just born weeks ago. I
had always loved babies,
I'd hate myself if
she fell. I hold her
close...her eyes open,
she stares at me for
a second only. So much
I could say about how
pretty her eyes are and
I wish I could know and
I guess I'll always wonder
what she thought of me
for that second, for that
one moment.

—Michael Johnson

I AM A HOUSE

I am a house
Not tall, not small
Somewhere in between
A house sometimes full of different people
People with different ideas
Some friends with each other
And some not knowing of the other
Sometimes the house is empty
Save one
Alone
No ideas
No dreams
Sometimes not even a key to open the door

—Michael Johnson

IT IS SO CRUEL

It is so cruel
It is sometimes sad
It is so mean
It is so big
It is hated by some people
It is your future
It is my future
It is seeing poverty
It is seeing luxury
It is having fun
It is having sorrow
It is seeing people come
It is seeing people go
It is having friends that care
It is having friends that lie
It is knowing that you're there
It is going and getting high
It is suffering for what you don't have
It is wasting all your precious time
It is trying to strive for that big climb
It is something that we don't understand
It is a thing that is so confusing
It is a question why I am here
It is an answer that I will never hear
It is something I will fulfill
It is a thing no one can steal
It is all mine and I can keep it
It is only as long as I can make it

—Benny Kyles

YELLOW

Yellow, as in:
the sun shining brightly,
traveling, heat. The beach
I am adventuresome.

—Yvonne Bush

BLACK

The stars sparking in the
sky at night
The color of some pretty girl's hair
The evening gown she wore to the prom
Her mother's shoes that
dazzled her feet
The wandering night
sparkled in her eyes

—Tonia McIntosh

JUST BELIEVING

I am the water of a tear
I am the warmth of the sun
I am the redness of an apple
I am the green grass of summer
I am the smell of freshness
I am the softness of cotton
I am the walk of the proud
I am the hotness of fire

You ask who am I?

I am the seed of all plants
I am the leaves of all trees
I am the water that waters the grass
I am all that is beautiful

You asked who am I

—Sonja Jackson

STAR DREAM

Standing on a planet, a light
in the distance, I see it's a
quasar and it's coming towards me.
As it passes I jump on its back,
closing my eyes to its blinding
bright light. I ride it back
to earth, to my home, to my bed.

—Marc Thomas Bey

WATCHING

Everyone's
in a trance,
thinking of
what to write,
figuring out
a good poem,
and watching
our substitute
miss Bright.

—Harry Thorpe

WINTER'S DUSK

At dusk the
people stiffen
in cold air,
sparrows are
fixed in their
nests, the
smoke from chimneys
fills the air,
the moon
creeps up
from beyond
the clouds.

—Robert White

I

I
Just Don't
care.
Malchanceux
as
I am.
Devastating.
I
Just Don't
care.

—Phillip Weems

THE LONG DAY

The day is long and weary,
The snow falls silent to the ground,
As I sit in the classroom waiting, waiting,
I watch the bell, I look at the clock
Thinking, thinking about the day.
As time goes past I wait
For a long day to go by.

—Michael Johnson

I'M

I'm in love
with Mina
the winter
feels like summer
the clouds
pass by
I am happy.

—Phillip Harris

WAKE

You sit, thinking about the person,
how you'll miss them, people come,
interrupting your thoughts, and say,
hello and how sorry they are.
Someone cries.

—Wayne Toles

THE LIVES OF LOVED ONES

I see trees
and falling leaves
I see birds
on a branch
in a nest
on a limb
with the babies
crying for freedom
wanting to fly
But Mom says
"Loved ones
I don't want
you to die!"

—Alicia Roberts

POEM

A tree a cloud
a loud bird singing rain

—Denise Jakckson

FAT PEOPLE

Some are sloppy, wobbly and mean.
Some smell, some don't.
I have never seen any human so large.
They sweat, they snore. Fat people, fat people,
what can I say. They sit around
and eat all day. They bounce so
happily in the spring.

—Elliot Hill

I REMEMBER

I remember my mommy,
a nice lady with a fat
tummy

She went away to bring
me a present and when
she came home all dressed
in Black,

she got in the car with
a smile on her face, a tear
in her eye. She said my
next one isn't going to die.

—Heidi Robinson

I REMEMBER

I remember the time
when I stopped and
floated in the water
all that I could see
was shadows of lights
and the water felt
like a bed
my mind just
floated like
a leaf on a
wave to
sleep

—Steve Hairston

I'M TONY

I'm Tony
I'm strong as a boar
I'm cooler than I believe
I'm alive
I'm smarter than the smartest
I'm cuter than cute itself
I'm finer than the finest
I'm soul itself
I'm colder than cold itself
I'm a dancer of my own sounds

—Tony Smith

PEOPLE

They are white, they are black,
they are brown. But it really
does not matter. But
sometimes it does.

—Gary Kennedy

THE BOY

He ran fast as a cheetah and
he jumped as high as a kangaroo,
he was as big as a tree,
but when he asked a girl out
she turned and laughed.

—Bruce Wagner

IN A ROOM DESPERATE

In a room desperate,
My friend has gone.
I'll never see him again.
Perhaps I shall see him
In the promised land.

—Tracy Cooper

I SAW

I saw trees and grass and shrubs
too much
too many flowers
too much earth
I saw people standing, sitting
around and looking blankly
from one to another
I saw black
and a progression
that I never want to see again

—Jennifer Adair

I CAN SEE

I can see my friends
just lying in the bed dead.
I could see them just getting up
then they get shot in the head,
and they are shaking, trying to
survive.

—Steve Hairston

A STREET

A gray sidewalk
the clappiting noise of shoes
smell of food
heat of the sun
the sounds of birds
buses, cars

—Christopher Pitts

WHAT I AM

I am human like the universe
I am like the brown of wheat
I am keen like a saw mill

My skin is smooth as
the air we breathe.
My personality is like
the back yard of earth.
I am what I be
and be what I am.

—Charles Williams

I REMEMBER

I remember where my great Aunt lived
there were always cows and horses and
there were watermelons on the ground
and my uncle was on the porch playing
his guitar and the wind would pass through
every so often
and smell the air from the grapes
in the South!

—James Quarterman

I am like a star shining
I am like a calm river at night
I am like an owl at night hunting
I am like a room in the dark
I am like a growing tree in an open field
I am like a fish in the sea
I am like a sun that don't shine

—Donnell Woodson

BLUE ROOM

In my blue room
close the door
for he shall not see who
comforts me

Wondering in the dark room
who will be my next love
be my only love my
next love

Starting all over
starting in the dark
all over again all
over

Let me take you through
the woods where the
blue wind
blows

—Carolyn Davis

I DON'T NEED NO LIGHT

I don't need no light

Don't you know I can see
through you

Need to be seen. But I don't
need no light

No need to be loud. Be
unique

Light. I don't need no light
to see through you

—Tina Crawford

THE END OF SCHOOL IS HARD

The end of school is hard.
It is like this because
You have exams to take.
Your mind is full of
So much studying and
Your memory is drawning
In education.
But when school lets
Out you forget about it
And when the next school
Year starts you have forgotten
It all.

—Tracy Williams

CONVERSATION

Conversation calm and cool
talking tall tales about tall
women while tossing a football
or dribbling a basketball or
just lying under a large
shaded cool tree drinking 7up.

—Lineal El-Amin

SHAW HIGH

Shaw High
is a so so place to be
and a wonderful place
to learn from but
it's also an igloo all covered with snow
with a courtyard leading to about three steel doors,
people walking around in they double-breasted coats,
they tweeded snow suits and
wraparound scarves and so forth.

But in the summer
it's like a trip to fashion show,
in the lounge, the tech, the vocational,
sitting on the grass, all over, nothing but flying colors,
guys and gals with they Hawaii shirts,
and skirts with little sandals to match
The fashion show.

—Yulanda Hayden

FIRST GRADE

The past is a faded and forgotten
dream. Full of monsters and bogeymen.
Like my first grade teacher with her goldfish glasses
and her pointy nose. She wore a size 18D in lady fashion.
Her hair was made from wool and her teeth of wood,
she had a wooden leg, and bone on the top of her hair.
That is a dream of what I remember
of my first grade teacher.

—Strauther Hosea

I AM

I am the Thought in most females' minds
I am a Hero in the eyes of the young
I am Elegant with my every move
I am the Opponent of every evil doer
I am the Point of every mountain
I am the Oz of all men
I am Loved by everyone
I am Impossible to predict
Could I be Superman?

—Theopolis Washington

JUNE LANGFORD BERKLEY
11 Blue Line Drive, Apt. E
Athens, OH 45701
(614) 592-2649

Elem. and Sec

June teaches in the English Department at Ohio University, Athens, and in the evening school at Marietta College, Marietta, Ohio. Her novella *Shannaganey Blue* was published by The University of Akron this year. She was Fiction-Writer-in-Residence at Shawnee State Community College in the fall of 1982 and has appeared as a storyteller and fiction reader throughout the United States. In addition, she gives workshops for teachers of writing, drawing on a background of experience as a high school English teacher and several years as a free-lance journalist. She has worked extensively with the Anit-Censorship movement and recently appeared in a nationally distributed film produced by the Association of American Publishers.

That letter about Mitty Groves was the first mail Dugans ever got, and I think it really did come because I wished for it on the evening star. I might have said a wish for Mitty himself—if I had known, if I had thought it was possible to get a child like that.

The winter before, after Mart Dugan helped at lambing time, I'd stood a long time at the front window, watching his single footsteps cross the meadow, winding home through hard packed snow. I'd watched, my face pressed against the frosty glass, his gray mackinaw was only a speck in the evening haze.

"Why don't Sarah and Mart have any children?" I'd asked, propping my elbows on the edge of the new quilt pulled tight on the long frame.

"Well, they just don't. Some people just never have any children." She never looked up from her quilting. "Don't lean on the frame."

"But maybe someday they'll have one," I'd answered, remembering how Sarah always laid her hand on my head when she gave me thick slices of warm bread with lots of butter.

"Well, no. Not after they're so old. People don't have any children after they get so old, Kate." She snipped the thread quickly and looked away. She never liked to talk about getting babies.

And that first warm spring night when my mother and I crossed the meadow and walked up Dugan's Run, I saw, next to ours in the thick tangle of last summer's weeds, their old mailbox with its half-hinged door agape like a rusty tongue in the gray vines. My mother closed it and I said, "They don't ever get any mail, do they? How's come they even have a mail box?"

"They just do," my mother said. She broke back the woody vines that crept along the rail fence.

"That's the same thing she said about having a child," I said to myself, walking slowly, watching every puddle for thin clouds of grey jelly that would mean frog's eggs—and tadpoles coming.

V.C.H.S.

The riotous roaring pep club
On the way to a freezing football game
And the strutting of the jocks after the victory
Over the suburb of Hamden
Congregated coaches meeting in the halls
Talking over last night's game.

Quiche flying from the singing French room
Astro blast 'em on the Spanish walls
Rumble of Mrs. Litter's mouth over mutilated Algebra books
The crack of half a yard stick from Mr. Caldwell's room
Silly Simmons singing sixties songs
"'Till daddy takes the T-bird away."

Creaky old floors, giant eye windows
Dark, creepy dungeon and a maze of concrete steps
Peeling chalkboards, black woodwork
Ever-winding spider webs on the multi-colored walls
Graffitized walls, unsanitized stalls

Thousand word essays for looking out the window
Closed life for chewing gum, lunch hour never ends
I.S.S. when you're caught skipping
Detention for talking in class
Or roaming the halls
Mr. Crow will whop you hard
For walking on the grass.

Going uptown to eat
Buying ski at nearest machine
Talking to friends, passing notes
Hoping it goes unseen
Meeting your Someone Special between classes
Remember, no physical contact.

This is our school — the good and the bad,
The musty walls and all,
The friends that delight, the teachers that fright
You can do what you want if you don't get caught
The jocks and their girls with crew-cuts and curls
Through the years, though it may change,
It will always be V.C.H.S.

—Lori Wright, Collen Casto, Missi Bethel,
Melinda Buskirk, Jill Booth

(Mr. Caldwell's class)

Kind of imprisoned here
Everything
I
Think about is
Horses

Joy
Often
Returns after school
Definitely
And
Never wants to return

Keith Jordan

These be three simple things
  Water in a river
Animals running in the woods
  Night time

—Pam Prater,
Laurie Ward

VC DREAM SCHOOL

Five-minute classes
Forty minute breaks
Video game rooms, ski pop
Student teachers, no work
Carpeted hallways and good
rock music in the rooms
No principals and no rules
No coaches for any sports
Olympic-size swimming pool
Beautiful blond girls everywhere
Air conditioned rooms and
Tinted windows, astroturf
everywhere so we can walk
on the grass whenever we want,
live AC/DC concerts in the gymnasium
during our lunch periods, and at
the end of the day we have a chauffeur-
driven limosine to take us all away.

—Brent Wright, Dough Thompson,
Rob Stewart

(Miss Nisely's class)

Living
In my life is
Sometimes
A blast but I am
Peaceful sometimes but
Really
Always want
To talk
Even
Right now!

—Lisa Prater

My
Everyday
Life
In
School is
Silly
Always
Happy
Until she gets
Nosy and
Talks a
Lot
Ever be a talker!
Yes!

—Melissa Huntly

FREEZING FOOTBALL GAMES

Those freezing football games all so cold
Sitting on the bleachers
Cheering for the almighty Vikings
And eating the unpopped kernals of popcorn
In the bottom of my bag.
Munching on a cold hotdog with frozen mustard
and catsup
Trying to keep warm by wrapping cold blankets
  around me
Yes, I'm freezing but I can't leave the
almighty Vikings.

Nelsonville has us down 14-13
But we shall come back
With our experts skills to overcome
With the help of the cheerleaders and our
crowd
We should easily have a win

—David Beyers, Matt Chesser

SPRING TUESDAY

Spring Tuesday out my window:
Telephone wires fight in the windy skies;
Pigeons rest on the bare branches of the
budding trees;
Robins ride the swinging wires
Below, the golden dandelions
Rest with satisfaction.

—Linda Collins, Chris Hale,
Susan Casto

These be three
Smelly things
The old rendering plant
The smell of the cafeteria's
green pizza

—Scott Arganbright, Greg Hughes

These be
three pretty things
the flowers, birds
beginning of spring
the living

—Vileta Barnett,
Kitty Shaffer

These be
Five banjo strings
Playing bluegrass music
Playing colorful chromatics
five strings

—David Huff

Hartford Junior High School
Resident poet: Anna Bishop

Dream Poems

I have a dream that
Someday I will become
the world's greatest baseball player
(even though I already am!)
I have a dream that
someday, someone will notice me,
and help me reach the top.
I have a dream that
when I reach my destiny,
I will have made a lot of people happy,
and keep my love
for the sport of baseball.

—Clarence Owens

I have a dream that
someday, I'll be famous lawyer,
and become very rich.
I have a dream that
I'll become SO RICH
that people won't even notice
that I'm BLACK!
I will become known all over the world,
known for being such a good lawyer!

—Michael H. Jackson

I have a dream that,
one day I'll live in success
as a surgeon, or a doctor,
and associate with the best.

Save human lives
while they're on the operating table
thinking they're gonna die,
to save them, I'll be able.

This is my preferred dream
of a lifetime.
Enjoying every minute of the day,
every minute of the nighttime.

—Andrea Wells

I have a dream that is only for me—
That all my wishes will come true,
and I'll never have to be blue.

My life will not fall apart—
like so many I've seen.
With the upbringing I have,
I know I can survive,
The terrible things this pitiful world
has to offer—
I know one thing for a fact,
That my mother loved me
and did what she thought was right.
She let me make mistakes!
That's the best way to learn
how to survive!!!

—Kim Jeter

Anansi Triplets

Anansi
is a West African Spider man
but he is not for real.

Anansi,
who was known to be a spider man—
who came from way back when!

—Samantha Corbin

Anansi
So very thin and tall,
don't be surprised if he climbs your wall.

—Roy V. Henderson

A BALLAD

One time while walking down the street,
I saw this pretty girl I wanted to meet.

I walked up closer to see her face—
Boy, oh, boy, was that a disgrace?

She was so ugly, short, and stubby,
I looked at her stomach—she was very chubby.

When she smiled (she was thinking of kissing),
She spread open her mouth—she had three teeth missing!

She turned around, didn't mean no harm,
And knocked me out with her underarm!

—Troy Gordon

Poems based on music—
"What's the Matter, World?"

What's the matter World?
I ain't got no job.

What's the matter World?
Need money for the Mob.

I just got to keep on giving
If I'm going to keep on living.

—Mark M.

What's the matter World?
I ain't got enough love,
I got too much hate.

What's the matter World?
I ain't got enough food,
I got too many people.

What's the matter World?
Think I'd rather die!!!

—Souleatha Graves

GUM BABY

Hey, Gum Baby,
How did you get here?

Some white man brought me,
And I fought all the way!

Hey, Gum Baby,
Why are you sticking on me?

I don't know—
I guess I'm just trying to be free.

Hey, Gum Baby,
You like being here?

It's not right to bring blacks
Over through the night.

Hey, Gum Baby,
Did they take away your pride?

No, man, but I'm still going to run
and hide!

—Tony McElroy

I'm as cheerful as a hyena.
I'm as skillful as a beaver.
I'm about as popular as a skunk.
I'm as talkative as nervous bird.
I'm as confident as a deer.
I'm as good looking as a premature swan.
I'm as smart as an owl.
I'm as good a money manager as Phillip Pirrup
I love freedom as much as new clothes.

—Wendy

I'm as cheerful as a child with a new toy.
I'm as skillful as a man with no fingers.
I'm as popular as a pony in a horse race.
I'm as talkative as a baby learning to speak.
I'm as confident as a person in a shark tank.
I'm as good looking as a baby with food all over
its face
I'm as smart as a 10th grader.
I'm as good a money manager as a six year old.
I love freedom as much as I love living.
Do you believe this?

—Mimi Kennedy

A dangled cigarette
From an old man's hand
Releases a wisp of smoke
To the dim light of the cafe.
The walls are dark.
and the comfort's there
Beneath the rough exterior
The sweating glass with golden beer,
The grease on the table,
The square legs of the chair,
The aged bartender...
All add to my adventure.

—Mark Streeter

A cup of coffee
A pillow
A book
Feeling emotions that are forgotten as the last
page is turned.
A time to spend alone with your imagination
and feel satisfaction.
Simplicity at its height.

—Barb Linstrom

A large, comfortable chair
A dim light, a soft pillow
Next to a bright fire
With a sleeping cat, curled in a ball
The sound of rain on the window
(Nothing to do during the afternoon)
And a good book.
But, the book is the key to discovery,
Prying the mind open, almost against it's will.
The rain stops, the cat awakes,
the fire flickers and goes out.
Any place at all is in the room
Then the cat stretches, yawns,
Goes back to sleep
And the rain begins to fall
Against the window.

—Sharon Pittenger

Southside Settlement
Canton

Mother Goose Conversion

Jack and Jill went up the hill
To puff a joint of dope.
Jill got so stoned
You could see her bones,
And Jack just played jump rope.

—Bill Floyd

CONVERSATION PIECE—Based on African Call & Response Pattern

What's inside a pencil?
Only words waiting to be written.
What's inside the sun?
A thousand killowatt smiles.
What's inside a flower?
Centuries of future flowers.
What's inside yourself?
Look in my eyes and tell me.
What's a devil?
The devil is the ocean.
What's the ocan, then?
What's the ocean, then?
The ocean is your teeth.
What if I smile?
You'll have a whale of a time!!!!

—Bill Floyd & Teresa R. (Adult Leader)

EARL BUTLER
1908 Timmonds Avenue
Portsmouth, OH 45662
(614) 353-5059

b. 1945
Elem and Sec

Earl attended the University of Hawaii and received a BA in English from Wright State University. He has worked as a reporter for the Dayton *Journal Herald,* a print shop artist, a field and mill hand, and works during the warm months as a landscaper. He was writing instructor and Chairman of Liberal Arts at the School of the Dayton Art Institute until its demise in 1975. Two limited edition collections of his poetry have been published; he was founder and editor of MINORITY REPORT magazine and founder of the Peach Mountain Poetry Festival. Recently his work has appeared in LIVE WRITERS, MAELSTROM, SPITBALL and other literary magazines.

THE TIE LOG

while searching for spare lumber over
near peebles   i hear my voice   like fog rain
bungling to explain that it seems a matter
of environment to me
            for instance
                  a grain
of ocean sand has storm force recalls a clatter
of hurricane gods to a sailor i know who's found
his knots & blocks & tackle pulling down old tabakker
barns lately
      and still the sea swells the clay ground
behind him
    yes environment
            sez my mud rain
honky drawl
    means these hardwoods get thicker
with age
    and it runs deep this hanging around
sawmills where the sweet-glow flesh of wild cherry
is sawed for subway crossties   sawed young & cherry

Earl Butler

Clay High School
Scioto County

THE SEASONS

Riding a bobsled
On a wintry white trail—
fastly going on

Trees are turning green
Lots of grass can now be seen,
Life returns to us

Time is passing now
In the summer's hot season—
Scorching July days

Watching the leaves fall
Amongst the autumn moonbeams—
ever falling down

—Dave Sexton
Grade 7

---

one day i saw cars
the next day i saw wrecked cars
they were foreign cars

—Tony Robinson
Grade 8

---

one day I saw a big fight
and the littest man won
and he went on having fights

—Bryan Moore
Grade 8

the lake was silent
ready to chill
a soft breeze sang
cool and brazen
color falls softly to the ground

—Kim Martin
Grade 10

SQUIRREL HUNTING

The woods are calm.
And the trees are still.
The squirrel hunter is quiet.
While he waits up on the hill.

The hill is his favorite place,
And he's at his favorite spot.
He doesn't wait a minute,
He's there at 5 on the dot.

He sitting there so quiet.
You could hear a twig snap.
He hears a cutting drop,
Then a limb crack.

He looks up.
And sees a huge red squirrel
Tearing through the trees.

His shotgun is very loud,
It has a mighty roar.
It echoes through the hills
and goes on forever more.

—Louie Minch
Grade 9

THE BEAST

You start up slow
going up and up, higher
you climb, into the clouds,
and you get to the top of a 40 foot drop.

So down you go, your hands are sweating,
your eyes in a glaze, up and down
and even upside down.
Your heart is throbbing
like it's going to bust.

When suddenly it's over
and you're back on your feet
going to find another thrill.

—Neil Clark
Grade 8

HARLEY DAVIDSON

cherry red chrome headers
98 miles an hour
tires melting
engine winding
headers red
hair blowing happy
sliding scared
clothes tearing
rubbing asphalt
kickstand in head

hello hog heaven

—Dave Braden
Grade 9

RIDE ON

she's a mean harley rider
with leathers and lace
she has a tattoo of an eagle
on her face

she has a panhead harley model 64
it's black and chrome
and a whole lot more
while she holds it to the floor

she'll ride on   ride on   ride on

she has leathers and skintight jeans
being a biker is in her dreams
and she'll be one some day

she'll ride on   ride on   ride on

—Sherman Martin
Grade 9

WALKING ON A SPRING DAY

walking through a meadow
scent of spring flowers
the grass is green
trees blooming

in the brook
steel calm glassy waters

there is a cool breeze blowing

—Herman Patrick
Grade 9

one flower stands alone.
it has no accompaniment
except the wind and the sun.
the three blend into a gentle
harmony. the one flower
stands alone.

—Noelle Horsley
Grade 9

My pen rolls along this line
Because it is a ball point pen.
It lives through many hardships:
like getting sat on & squashed.
I dedicate this paper to it
So it can have some fun.

—Pat Mullins
Grade 10

BLANK

without a thought
nothing to say
no way to say
no way to be expressed
nothing to express
no meaning to anything
TOTAL emptiness

—Lynn Boynton
Grade 11

CONTEMPLATIONS OF A LUNATIC

railroad tracks across my arm
bumping across my veins.
I feel the rumbling in my soul,
like the emptiness of a cereal bowl.

the black smith hung clint eastwood
who walked the paper moon,
trumpet blasts announced prince charles
and the fork ran away with the spoon.

Daffy Duck did the minuete,
old abe looks sternly on,
he chewed his mail pouch chew,
and spit the juice in the hippo's mouth
as he began to yawn.

I cut my arm while shoving it,
and it began to bleed,
the bald man has my shirt on,
I drained my stein of mead.

This is the end of my ravings,
my rantings are at end,
I'm still as crazy as a loon,
will you please by my friend?

—David Pruitt
Grade 9

KILL MY TEACHER

She lashes out tooth and nail
Informs me that I may fail,
I've delved below the passing scale—
Kill my teacher. Kill my teacher.

She doesn't care how I feel,
Her Vixen mouth begins to squeel,
I ask myself, "what's the deal?"
Kill my teacher. Kill my teacher.

A loathing for the school days,
My mind's engulfed in an endless maze,
I think her house I'll set ablaze,
Kill my teacher. Kill my teacher

—Brian Conley
Grade 12

---

sails flying in wind
ocean currents carry
lonesome ships away

—Michelle Stidham
Grade 11

---

spotted brown fawn stands
alone
against green & blue sky

—Michelle Stidham
Grade 11

A MODERN ADVENTURE

The man begins his journey
blind and determined,
doomed to fail.

Thick foliage surrounds him
chokes him, blinds him
jungle sounds envelop him
pervade him, deafen him.
onward he stumbles.

Through the oft-trodden marshes
dodging the slippery yet adhesive vines
animal sounds continue to buffet him
attempting to drain his will.
onward he stumbles.

The man no longer remembers
why he began his trek
too late to go back now
he must reach the other side,
onward he stumbles

The animals reveal themselves
with translucent facades
impeding but never touching him
slowing but never stopping him.
onward he stumbles.

The man continues on his journey
knowing his attempt is in vain
while terrible eyes keep watching, mocking
the man weeps for himself.
onward life stumbles—

forever onward.

—Wes Miller
Grade 12

COMPUTER INFORMATION

Hold again, Hold again,
Hold it one more time.
Hold again, hold again,
Hold it one more time.

Too much information running through my brain,
Too much information driving me insane.

People don't care
They walk right by
The boy with the computer brain.
They just want him for programming
They won't let him sleep at night
But the cold computer keeps him warm

Too much information running through his brain,
Too much information, driving him insane.

Hold again, Hold again,
Before it blows my mind.
Hold again, hold again,
Before it blows my mind.

—Shelly Crum
Grade 11

THE ETERNAL SPONGE

Never prepared, always vigilant, finding what he lacks,
His tentacles protrude, but encounter no facts,
His lust for objects insatiable, a gaping duct
A garbage can, a magnetic man, a living suction cup.

His locker is an abyss, a leaping hissing mound.
Fossils lie within it, and unending lot & found.
He knows not what he does, to him it's just a game.
I borrowed this book from someone,
I don't recall his name.

—Brian Conley
Grade 12

THE DOORS

Scenes on the wall
painted by others,
Views from their mental screens
of places, people
become real to us.

Closed minds are wasted space,
unused, empty places
where nothing ever dares
to enter
guarded by obsolete ideas
They kill the soul.

—Dirk Sullivan
Grade 11

HALE CHATFIELD — b. 1936

13560 Old State Road — Elem and Sec

Huntsburg, OH 44046

(216) 632-5672

Hale is associate professor of English and poet in residence at Hiram College where he founded the HIRAM POETRY REVIEW. He is the author of six volumes of poetry and one volume of short fiction. In addition, he is the recipient of creative writing fellowships from the National Endowment for the Arts and the Ohio Arts Council. In 1967, with a grant from the National Endowment for the Humanities, he designed and directed a summer workshop for teachers of poetry. He is also director of a consulting firm, North Star Associates.

INSOMNIA: *June, 1982*

Lord
you have given me words
to be afraid:
possibly and late at night
if if

because and *maybe.*
so that I am shaken in the dark
pulled to folly
as if I were capable of tides
and the moon moving across my sleep
has nothing but names so that I surge
toward it as it passes over me
the hand of a magician,
a bishop, so that I roll from east
to west drawn even in my sleep
by names: *moon*

and *terrified* and *too much:*
the girl at my side is almost my age
now, forty-five. She is getting closer
each year as you turn me toward her

passing your word over me
stars stars which alarming and lovely
shudder in the sky
at my feet

little voices of God
and I am glad, perhaps,
because I am weeping
while angels crumple the word *menace*
and it thunders. Just a little.
And rains.

—Hale Chatfield

Reprinted by permission of the editors of THE HIRAM POETRY REVIEW.

North Road School
Howland

UP IN MY MAGIC ROOM

Up in my magic room
I have a horse in my room.
It is very speshel to me
because it can do things
for me. It can do my
homework and It can drive my car. Nobody
nose abote it because It is magic.

—Scott Justice

Mines Elementary School
Howland

I live in an old dark house. I have a secret
about my room. It is a room you would always
dream of having. It is red, white and blue.
It is so magical, all you have to do is say ala
casam and then make a wish and it will come
true after you make a wish just lay down on the
bed and go to sleep and dream about three stars
sleep three hours every hour take one star away,
when there gone you will wake up and your wish
will be right beside you it can do a whole
bunch of other things but there a real secret.

—Gino Luccarelli

In my house there is a magic room. No one knows about it but me I wanted to know what was in the room. So one night I open it up. And when I open it there was another world.

So I stepped inside and it smelled horrible.

I turned around to go out and there stood a ten foot man. I told him how horrible the smell was. So he said "I can fix that". And he cut off my nose. Then I ran to the door open it and went out and then felt my nose and it was back on.

—Molly Lambert

I opened my door this morning, and I saw a giant peace of chalk. He said good morning my name is white because I am a white peace of chalk. And I said what are you doing here? He had no reply. But he did say let's go to a school and draw on the board. I said forget it and slamed shut the door. And went to sleep.

—Cathy Nigro

Telephone Poem

8 How do you like to eat red hearts?
5 Everybody likes to eat them.
6 Anybody could try to eat them.

7 They may find out that there good
3 However maybe not.
5 Elephants love to eat them.
8 Rudolph tried it once and got pink eye.

—Heather Lambert

Pantoum

1 I have never been to Niagra Falls.
2 We were going by car.
3 A big, big, big car.
4 So big it could hold an elephant.

2 We were going by car.
5 My car.
4 So big it could hold an elephant.
6 Wow!

5 My car.
7 I like my car.
6 Wow!
8 Said my friend.

7 I like my car.
3 A big, big big car.
8 Said my friend.
1 I have never been to Niagra Falls.

—Johnny Russell

---

1 I saw a man with a chain hanging from his hand.
2 I thought my eyes were not working.
3 And what did I see?
4 Nothing at all.

2 I thought my eyes were not working.
5 When I saw the man again he had a dog with
the chain.
4 Nothing at all
6 Then I saw a dog with a man on a chain.

5 When I saw the man again he had a
dog with the chain.
7 I know my eyes are not working.
6 Then I saw a dog with a man on a chain.
8 And I said Oh no!

7 I know my eyes are not working.
3 And what did I see?
8 And I said Oh no!
1 I saw a man with a chain hanging from his hand.

—Anonymous

---

1 Marcy ate a frog
2 It was big
3 It was big as her face
4 She got sick

2 It was big
5 And also was fat
4 She got sick
6 Again

5 And also was fat
7 With green eyes
6 Again
8 She ate more frogs

7 With green eyes
3 It was big as her face
6 Again
1 Marcy are a frog.

—Anonymous

Parenthetics

The shoes I was standing in
Blew the cat up into
A pink pencil exploded
A rainbow disintegrated
Into two tiny pieces
Then thosand pieces of brown fur
Burst into tiny strands of brown yarn

—Molly Lambert

Eating paper is not good
Pencils lead blows up in
When you wash dishes
Glass people blow up
My bubble blew up
in Green Houses
You get soap in your eyes
Your face at 12:00 midnight
for your health or your tummy

—Paula Sapp

Park Layne Elementary
Resident poet: Horace Coleman

Fog is a cloud down low
It's all white
There's kind of like smoke in it
You can't see houses
You can't see a white cat
It feels like cotton, furry
It feels like snow-cold
In the fog you feel windy, froze
You can see your bus

—Collaboration
Mrs. Patrick's 2nd Grade

Fog is cold
It's like breeze
It's put together thick

—Michael Anderson
Grade 2

IMAGINATION

As I begin to think
All I can see is little funny pictures
Of socks, shoes, and the kitchen sink.
I start to dream of people, and places
And things to see
When my little funny pictures come back to me
I realize it was all inside me
It was just my imagination

—Marie Macionowski
Grade 5

The Plains Indians follow the Buffalo
and they have the teepee and
they call the babies pappooses
horses pull trovois
and they used the skin to make
moccasins and vests and pants
and smoke peace pipes
and when they take the skin
off the buffalo then they eat the meat
If I could have an Indian's name
it would be Running Fox

—Elba Watson
Grade 3

You cant describe nothing
it looks like nothing
nothing sounds like nothing
nothing is nothing
nothing makes me feel nothing
nothing makes me happy
nothing makes me sad
nothing is nerve racking
nothing eats like nothing

—John Phares

Indians are as big as the Pilgrims
The Indians are as mean as the Pilgrims
But the Indians sleep on the ground.

—John LaPois
Grade 3

BRAINS

icky   bloody
smooshy   clay
smelly   tasty
yuck   sick
interesting   gross
worms   skinny
tubes   horrible
veins   brains

—Mrs. McKnight's class

Birthday
Better than other days
Ice cream
Ready for dessert
Tasty
Happy
Daddy
Astronomically fun
Year older

—Anthony Part
Grade 3

LIMERICK

There was a young fellow named Kent
Who fell in a tub of cement.
When it hardened and dried,
It was cozy inside,
But they said you will have to pay rent.

—Jeremy Evans

WHEN I GROW UP

I will go places
I will drive race cars
I will be a trucker
I want a motorcycle
I want a big house with
ten doors and two storeys in it
I want a semi
I want a four-wheel drive
People will have rockets
on their backs
I would fly to work
At work, it would be like
semis with rockets under them
I would be a house destroyer

—Charlie Roberts

Donnell Jr. High School

THE BIG GAME

The game was in the gym.
It looked like they were
watching a fight—
People screaming like maniacs—
Standing, running, sitting, cheering,
Pushing people off the benches.
The team was tired, sweaty and mad.
They scored a lot of points
  but they tried too hard.
They looked like wilted flowers.
When the buzzer sounded
  everybody dropped their heads.

—Mrs. Grener's 8th Grade

THE BILLION DOLLAR BOXING MATCH

It's like a boxing tournament
Marathon in one corner
Mobil in the other
It's like Sugar Ray vs. Roberto
15 rounds of sweaty battle
The Supreme Court is the referee
They're greedy
Mobil got in the first punch
Marathon had a quick comeback
There's a sold-out crowd of 37,000
Smoking cigars, wearing red, backing Marathon
Now it's like a tag team match—
Marathon tags U.S. Steel
The crowd's excited, getting out the beer
They're duking it out in
  the middle of the 10th
And Mobil's on the ropes....

—Mrs. Gore's 8th grade

THE WAR FOR POWER

It's like a bad dream
people are mad
you could fry an egg
on their head—
for oil, for power,
to control lives & jobs—
people are helpless as a baby
locked in a closet
Findlay would be an empty jar
like a dustbowl without any dust
but that baby's going to
grab some clothes
stack them up
grab that doorknob
and turn that sucker open!

—Mrs. Gore's 8th Grade

Images

A rainy day is...
like a bucket of water
thrown on your plan,
stronger than any downer
you can buy.

—Anonymous

Money is as scarce as a pink cat

—Liz Ladd

A library is like
a morgue full of books

—Doug Garner

A rock concert is as loud as
a car with a hole in the muffler

A library is like a quiet
stream in a deep woods,
the air is like the air in space
with no gravity

—Jaci Martin

Contrasts

Here it's quiet as an unoccupied building
There it's like jungle paradise
Here I feel like a routine schedule
There I feel as surprised as the weather

—Dewight Smith

Here it's gloomy like a gray sky.
There it's peaceful as a whisper.
Here I feel like garbage being ground up.
But there I feel like a feather
being plucked from a turkey.

—Jodi Ernest

Here it's—as boring as a 10-hour opera
There it's—interesting as an alien planet
Here—I feel alone as a hermit
But there—I feel as wanted as
a missing puzzle piece.

Amy Huffman

Here it's as if I was
tied down all day.
There it's like a fantasy world.
Here I feel like
a person in prison.
But there I let myself go
like fishing line from a reel.

—Bill Mullen

Rain

Worms drowning in the mud.
Lying on driveways.
Climbing slowly for their last breath.
Hoping it will soon be over.
So do I.

—Ron Davis

When the rain falls
it depresses me,
When the mud forms
it delifts me,
When it looks so bleak
it saddens me,
When the worms come out
it sickens me.
When the wind roars
it scares me,
When the flood comes
it terrifies me,
When it all goes away
it relieves me.

—Bernadette Moore

RAINY DAY

I sit in my room and listen to
the rain hit the roof which sounds like
stars falling from the sky. And when I
look out my window the rain looks like
tear drops from the trees which
cover the ground in its own special way.

—Ryan Heldman

The streets are slick and shiny
puddles disappear when cars pass
drops bounce and bead on the hood
a rainbow of umbrella rush down
the sidewalks.
Day becomes night.

—Doug Sprouse

LOVE IS PAIN

People say love is like a rose,
I say love is like a knife.
It doesn't attract you,
It attacks you.

It sneaks up on you and
Stabs you in the back.
You feel it chipping at your bones,
Chipping your bones down to
toothpicks.

If you ever feel this kind
Pain you may believe you're in love.

—Michelle Swihart

The Most Evil Thing

Being caught in a storm
  and the power goes off.
Having a terrible dream and
  you are the one who gets killed.
Finding something in your bed
  such as the book you put in
a few hours ago.
The most evil thing is opening
  your closet door and finding
your little brother standing
  right in front of you.

—Doug Williams

AUTHOR'S CONCEPTION:

no why or reason,
no cause or effect,
no present or future
no falsity or truth,
no understanding or knowledge
all is predictable,
death,
the supreme logic,
the void.

—Chris Schultz

AND ON THEY GO

At first all it was, was a cloud of dust
With the appearance of a storm.
As it got closer, it formed a wall
Stretching for miles and miles.
What could it be?
A stampede of angry animals?
It got closer and the sound of machinery could
  be heard.
Could it be someone to help me and my unit?
The closer it got, the clearer I could see
  the gun turrets.
The sound of marching was closing in.
Suddenly it stopped.
We started yelling for help.
They circled around us.
What were they doing?
We then realized the war was closing in.
They started shooting at us like wild game.
We stood helpless.
Their tanks rolled over us.
Bones could be heard crunching.
They took our valuables,
Stripped us,
and then they went on to slaughter others.
And on they go...
And on they go...

—Ken Laube

ME

I may not be big
But surely that will change

I may not be wise
But some day I will know

I may not be cute
But that will also change

I look up to you now
And that is rightfully so

I will also be measured one day
But not by what others might say

The only measurement you see
Is the one I feel about me.

—Bill Mullen

IF I LOVE YOU

If I love you,
  I must be part of you.
And to be part of you,
  I must not be things
That are not you.
  I must leave behind
The ugly passions, the imagination
  of my jealous mind.

—Michelle Ruiz

DARKNESS

D arkness
A bsence of colors
R oars of silence
K ingdom of blackness
N ight without light
E erie, another world
S hadows in your mind
S omething beyond imagination.

—Tom Hoppe

PHASES

When I was five, I had a play gun
Playing with kids under the midday sun.
"I'm gonna shoot ya," said one kid to me.
My plastic gun by the maple tree.

When I was twelve, B-B guns were the fad
Going hunting with my grandpa and Dad.
"Shoot the squirrel," said my pops to me.
My B-B gun by the maple tree.

When I was seventeen, Korea was the place
Shooting Koreans face to face.
"Do your country proud!" said the Colonel to me—
Hiding with rifle, behind a maple tree.

When I was twenty-two, back in the States,
Memories of friends who had met their fates.
"I'll call the final shot," the choice up to me.
My coffin was made from a maple tree.

—Andrea Goetz

Brooke, Farrah, and Sandra Dee
They all have pizazz
But that's not for me

Burt, Robert, and James Bond
All have appeal
But they always hang around
  with some dumb blonde

They all have big houses
Where they sit around
  the pool and chat
But I just want someplace
  to be proud where I
  can hang my hat

Stars are glamorous, rich
and all that
But I'd rather just be me
Surrounded by family,
  friends, and cat

—Jackie Blem

MAD MAN

Mad man
from hades
clutching a skull
carved from wood
Mad man
with medieval
thoughts
He'll take
your life
if you
betray your
mind

—Mark McKitrick

WATER FALLS

when water comes from the rocks
it's scratching and tearing at everything
in its path; then when it falls it falls with
the grace of a bird; when the water hits it
looks like
someone falling right on their face

—David Kutschbach

THE WAR

Men fighting
falling over one another
death
shooting
loud noises
mourning
sadness
sickness and wounds
caring, killing
when it's done
and fighting has stopped
the war of memories goes on.
Inside your head

—Andy Rutledge

RAGE

Building inside me until it seems
I can't hold it in any longer.
Every single minute gets worse,
Grows more tinny, depressing.
But I must keep it in
And pretend that everything is
fine.
Sometimes pretending helps
sometimes it makes things worse
Of course Mondays are always
Negative
It's been a bad one.

—Pam Buis

A BRIDGE

a road to life,
an escape to
reality.
Death on either
side.
A place to continue
your destiny.

—Sue Harrington

THE WIND

The wind has feet
that quickly move.
It walks over the ground.
I love how it skips the green grass.

—Scott Rittner

The wind has strong blows.
It steals your clothes
off your line.

—Paul M.

The wind has arms
that slowly pounce.
It goes into the trees.
I hate how it does
that freezing work.

—Chris Frantz

If i heard ghost sounds
I'd scream!
I'd tell my sister
to tell my Dad
to get something to kill the ghost.
I'd put on my Frankenstein costume—
put my green teeth in my mouth
and chew the ghost up.

—Afternoon kindergarten

Haikus

Birds all flying
They're free as the mountain peaks
Flying so graceful

—Tracy N.

Watch the butterfly
Flying so high in the air
Come sit here with me

—Abbi

PAC MAN

Munching and crunching
He munches bunches of dots
He is a maze craze

—Jim A.

The wind has hands that move softly.
It floats into the car.
I hate how it freezes
the long feet off of you.

—Nathan

The wind has eyes
that see weird.
It looks under the building.
I hate how it sees the short people.

—Lisa Hardwick

Indian Valley School

THE TIGER

Behind these bars I sit
wasting my life away
Behind me is a small dark pit
They feed me once a day
I only become older
Shorter of breath
Each day is even colder
One day closer to death

—Holly Hood

EARTH

Earth is like a can of sardines,
everyone's packed tightly in.
We're eating like pigs, taking our
cocaine and drinking vodka and gin.

These are busy streets, honking horns and wars
going on all the time.
With the gasoline shortage, and inflation, nothing's
worth a Tinker's Dime.

All of these problems together,
the world is a glutton.
The only solution I can find,
is let Reagan push the button.

—Todd McKee

Wilson Vance Elementary
Resident Poet: D. Steven Conkle

If I were a rainbow...

I'd sit around up in the sky all day
I'd look like a big slide out on a white playground
I'd look like an umbrella that someone had opened on
a sunny day,
And I'd look like a painted turtle crawling across
the sky.
And I'd look like the sky was saying "ok"
And I'd be the sky's ankle.

—Kindergarten

If I were the Winter...
I'd fall down onto the ground
And everything would be snow white
The world would look like a white horse
walking in the snow.
And if I were the Winter...
I'd blow the caterpillers right off the trees.
If I were the Winter...
People would give me money and I'd spend it
all on food —like grass
I'd eat the green skin off and make the grass brown.

—Kindergarten

WINTER

Among of white come swirling snow
It looks like a pillow fight when it comes
  along in December.
It is really nice in some ways too.
I like it a lot.
I can make a big white snowman or a
Big white snow fort.
Then you can see sometimes the
  wind get too rough and it knocks
  it down, then I rebuild it again.
Then I go inside and watch the wind come
  again and knock it down.

—Tricia McKinniss
Grade 2

WHAT"S SO BIG ABOUT WINTER?

Mom says bundle up
Mom says don't pull down icicles
You might get poked in the eye.
Mom says look at the pretty pine trees
And I say big deal.
Mom says wear your mittens and hat
Mom says put your boots in the garage
Mom says go blow your nose
Mom says go sit by the fire
Mom says go to bed early tonight
Mom says go hang up your snow mobile suit
Mom says go put on your sweater
Or get a blanket
And I say I hope winter is over soon.

—Jane Barchent
Grade 3

THIS IS JUST TO SAY...

I'm sorry I hit my brother
with a bat on his head.
Forgive me.
It looked funny how he made
a face like an ape
And a lion mixted together.
He was so funny I started
to laugh.

—Patricia Hrencecin

MY IMAGINATION

I woke up thinking what a yucky place Findlay is. Then I walked out on our rickity, rackity old grey porch to sit and think. All of a sudden, I was in Paris. It smelled of fresh fruit and perfume. There were belly dancers with silky clothes and royal people watching them. Then I was in Hawaii where hula dancers were doing their dances for tourists. I can smell the food being cooked and roasted for a luau. Then I went to a field in Utah. The air smelled even better than Paris or Hawaii. It's fragrance was made of flowers swaying in the gentle breeze and butterflies gathering nectar from roses and tulips. Then I woke up back in boring Findlay and rested my imagination for next time.

—Trisha Schubert
Grade 5

THE WILD GEESE

I hear the sound of the wild geese.
I dash outside and look into the sky.
Through the trees I see the great V's
of geese
Soaring above the clouds on their way
south.
They are as uniformed as an army
They make an unmistakable honking
sound
On their journey.
I stare in amazement.

—Colin Walker
Grade 6

THE EAGLE

It is a legend soaring overhead
With eyes as sharp as carpet tacks
searching for his dinner.
A little mouse runs through a field
and only he can see it
He swoops down like a bomb from
a plane,
And eats the tiny mouse for
his meal.

You'd better enjoy this view while
you can
The eagles might not be here
tomorrow.

—Sally Lodico/Grade 6

BACKYARD FOREST

My backyard has many trees
Shading me, making condominiums for birds
It's bark, like a sweater, protecting it.
It's branches like arms protecting animals.

—Phillip Ragland

THOU

Thou rain thou sunshine thou rainbow
Whatever arth thou likes arth thou likes
Arth thou you are gone whose you quote,
You are thou and thou and unquote,
dolk is the magic and mysterious word
for a thou who seeks the passion, hate,
and love, although it is hard to under-
stand, to quote, it is so that passion
hate and greed are to most evil that
thou controls you are doomed. You can
escape but of course you die and greed
and carsin will fill your brain of
HORROR.

—Chunk Kim
Grade 5

SPACE INVADERS

The Space Invaders are coming.
You can hear their footsteps
Coming closer getting louder.
You shoot at them, they shoot at you.
You can't beat them
Even if you shoot them all.
More come down.
Like players onto a football field,
Charging, charging
Until they blow you up.
Then they will take your money.
Taking quarters like pickpockets
Until you don't have any money at all.
Then you leave, unhappily,
Thinking to yourself
You've wasted your time;
You've wasted your money!

—Mark Shelton
Grade 6

JOHN D. ENGLE, JR. b. 1922
170 Stacy St. Elem and Sec
West Liberty, KY 41472
(606) 743-7576

John has had over a thousand poems published in such magazines as *The Christian Science Monitor* and *The Saturday Evening Post*. His books include *Laugh Lightly, Sea Songs, Modern Odyssey,* and a one-act play, *The Charm*. He lectures widely at high schools, colleges, and writers' and teachers' conferences, and is the recipient of numerous awards.

TO A YOUNG RELUCTANT POET

Although the spider brain
may have an unlimited
supply of web to spin,
there may not be
an unlimited amount
of time
for spinning.

Spin,
then,
thin
geometric
webs of dream-thought
on shrubs,
fences,
and trees.

Weave,
because you must,
your immediate meaning
so that dew
and the morning sun
will reveal
the perfect pattern
of your beauty,
the delightful design
of your visual poetry,
the mathematical mystery
of your love.

—John D. Engle, Jr.

(Originally published in THE COLUMBUS DISPATCH)

I AM

I am a mountain
proud and tall.

I am a cloud,
free to roam.

I am a boulder,
not to be pushed.

I am a river,
taking different paths.

I am a cornered animal,
when hurt.

I am a bird,
with closed wings.

—Mike Bensinger

I AM

...like a river with calm
cool glistening water.

a river that flows gracefully
away as though it were
riding on air.

a river that can be soft,
but hard

a river that can destroy and
save

a river as I and I as a
river

—Bill Binner

EXPERIENCING AN ORANGE

Slipping into an unfamilia daze,
Trying to escape the skepticism,
Entering the growing pores,
Astounded by the infinite trails.
Tasting the sweet surprise of a
  once familiar object,
Ignorant of the fact that
what I'm touching is an intricate poem
Awed by the wondrous matter before me
Taking a last lingering look,
Wishing to dwell a bit longer,
Knowing I must go
Slipping back to reality
Opening my eyes and realizing
  in just 2 or 3 minutes I experienced
A world of fascination.

—Jodi Elliott

THE WORLD OF ORANGE

The mysterious hole I slipped through
  leads to a pearly kingdom
  only a mind could pass to.
I followed a sweet, steep path
  to the Inner Chamber —
  curved columns
  of pearl and orange delight.
It was gloriously radiant
  to my sight.
And the smell
  was freshly, heavenly.
Sixteen crystal, amber pink columns
  eight jeweled seeds...
Then I took my last glance—
  at the last chance
  of the Celestial World
  inside an orange.

—Mei Li Evans

CATS

Cats are
sorcerers that
reside in a foreign body
with which they cast
their spells

—Michel Lautermilch

SUNRISE

The sun was once
a hot yellow topaz
on the finger of God
that was jolted from his earthly body
after his christening
and sent to the heavens
in remembrance

—Robin Dimling

ILLUSIONS

Illusions prevent
the insane from returning,
the sane from leaving.

—Anne Courtney

PARADOX (GRANDPA)

Though his body ages
 and weakens and shrinks,
His mind sharpens and
 builds up its strength.

Outside an old man
Inside a boy.

—David Worrell

Kyger Creek High School
Gallia County

HATE GROWS

Hate grows on hate
It grows until it takes
Complete control of the host's mind.
Hate Kills.

—Ed Rollins

PARADOX

Paradox is a word I never knew
It means half false and half true.

Some things might look the same to you
And yet they are different too.

Even though they have the same name
Don't be fooled if the colors the same.

Things are very different indeed
But you must look them over carefully.

When I get an orange V don't really see
If I picked the orange or the orange picked me.

There was a poet in our class today
And he tested us in a very unique way.

He showed us how different an orange can be.
From when you just look at it, and when you study
it carefully

—Rhonda London

I have a thought but I can't
express it.
Paradox
I have a feeling but I can't
put it into words.
Paradox
I have a dream but I can't share it.
Paradox
I have a life but I'm dying
everyday I live.
Paradox

—Susan Roush

HOW DOES A TREE BLOOM?

As winter ends
Days grow longer.
Nights get warmer;
Rain feeds the tree.
The tree comes out of its long sleep
Every thing's in slow motion.
Each day the tree seems fuller;
Buds speak out.
They seem to get a little bigger each day.
Time passes.
Everything is still
Then before you know it,
The tree is in full bloom.

—Kenny Coughenour

PEOPLE

Have you ever observed people walking
down a quiet street?
They seem to sway like trees
in the wind.
Just like an endless motion
of poetry.

—Terri Corbin

Kyger Creek Junior High School

Clouds how white they are
And how grey they can get on
A stormy midnight

—Cherie Johnson

MARC HARSHMAN
Bowman Ridge
RD #1, Box 52-A
Glen Easton, WV 26039

Marc holds degrees from Bethany College, Yale University, and the University of Pittsburgh. His first collection recently won a national competition sponsored by State Street Press and will be published in 1983. He has also recently been invited to read at the Manhattan Theatre Club in NYC. His poems have appeared in many periodicals in the U.S. and England, including POETRY NOW, IRONWOOD, POETRY NORTHWEST, and QUARTERLY WEST. His work will be included in the Appalachian poetry anthology to be published by the University of Mississippi Press. He is also an active storyteller (often in tandem with his wife Cheryl) and has conducted programs for all ages, including an appearance on KDKA-TV, Pittsburgh.

BESIDE COUNTY 303

The huge animals of trees
lift their shadows
across the still plain.
Inside the thick cloud of leaves
a thousand dreams,
a thousand small lives are
waiting for light, waiting
while out here the wind
is an almost silent bird,
a reason for what is
heard but can't be found:
that cut loop of wire I thought
hung near the gate, the leaves
crackling like fieldmice
hurried from bed, the animal
that sings one note
once an hour, here, then there, then
I'm not sure where it goes
losing itself like I do
in this large room of night;
and so I settle my back against a post
and continue the wait,
continue with darkness and questions,
wondering how long the light is,
what it will mean when it comes,
and in that darkest purple of the last night
know again how little there is to know,
know that soon enough the sky
that holds this large land,
its blue prairie, these black elms & brush,
will clear its way into light
and all the hidden, tiny engines of blood
will shine with fire and sing
and know nothing about wondering,
know nothing beyond mysterious need.

—Marc Harshman

French Art Colony
Adult Residency

COLLABORATION #1

Steamy days
Stinking ice
Overhead, a plane
Stone in rings of water
The frogs are sleeping

COLLABORATION # 2

Anything, any line in life,
you will use in your cheap poems but
while the ink is still wet
too late already to give
rise to some idea now omitted,
too soon to begin again.

WORDS

White and huge, he is my dog.
"Come, Sam, come here!"—
his one eye blue, the other one is brown,
he turns to scrutinize,
to see, if really I mean it,
and if I need him,
on his own choosing,
then he comes.

When you asked, "How would you
call him in your native tongue?"
Translate the words? Is there
a translation? "Tule, Pauka,
tule siia!" and he
lifted eyes—both brown
and loving as he came.

How do you translate the past
and say it in the words?
He was, just like Sam,
white and huge,
and he, too, was my dog.

—Vilma Pikkoja

Embracing chunks of life,
trying to convey the experience
in thick black words
on a cold white page,
failing
because
words can't breathe,
won't bleed
and don't whimper
in the dark.

They lay there,
impotent fossils,
barren husks,
dropped spoor,
not the real thing at all,
not the rustle
in the weed,
nor the shrill screech
of the wild boar.

—nan mykel

OBSERVATION ON AFFECTION

Whoever said that
absence makes
the heart
grow fonder,
never went
anywhere.

—Jena Harper

FAMILY

The flagstones in her garden path
are all but covered now.
The grass has creeped in around them,
invading...so tall,
that you have to part it and look closely
to even see the familiar pink and gray
that used to glisten in the afternoon sun.
She took such pride in that walk...
But...Mrs. Whittier's gone.

It's as if...the flowers know it, too.
Though the dianthus and carnations, on spindley necks,
still struggle to keep their heads above the weeds.
They come back every spring to bob and watch.
Hoping to catch some glimpse,
of her in her tattered sun-bonnet down on her knees.
Weeding,
weeding and talking, just above a whisper,
words intended only for her flowers and flagstone.
Touching, each one a special thing.

Oh, the neighbors will miss her,
Friends will miss her. . .
But no one will miss her like the flowers
and flagstone,
they were family...

—Jeanne Hill

TRIP TO POMEROY

Middle-aged bleached me
in a used yellow Gremlin
heading up Route 7
on Wodens Day,
slow truck in front, burdened, toting
sixteen logs that slip
toward the front, inside
their iron chains,
sixteen logs from the forest,
leaving sixteen stumps
behind.

At eight-twenty a.m. on
May five, nineteen eighty-two, in
Appalachia, decade
of Brooke Shields,
century of Ann Frank,
millenium of St. Joan,
a mud-spattered Ohio
license hangs beneath
rought cut faces
of former trees,
somewhere, pressed
between yesterday and
tomorrow on the long
journey to the mill.

—nan mykel

TERRY HERMSEN b. 1950
Route 1, S.R. 603 Elem and Sec
Plymouth, OH 44865
(419) 687-3085

Terry is originally from Michigan and received a BA from Wittenberg University. He has been publishing in such magazines as DESCANT, SOUTH DAKOTA REVIEW, CINCINNATI POETRY REVIEW, HIRAM POETRY REVIEW, and PIG IRON. In the fall of 1982, Terry was poet-in-residence for the Springfield Arts Council, working with senior citizens, inmates, and a women's group. He organized and narrated six radio programs about contemporary poetry, produced and broadcast by WYSO-FM, a public radio station in Yellow Springs.

THE ETERNAL

We have seen them
We know their forest
We don't know how they survive

We know *they* have seen *us*
That they want nothing to do with us
That they have given up names

The first explorers returned rich as doctors
Things changed
Then they didn't come back at all

We were amused
Was it better, or worse
Our whole fate hung on that pin

We shut down the factories
We shut the newspapers
We listened

It was very still

—Terry Hermsen

It looks like a forest of ice
covered with a blanket of clouds.
Darkness creeps up in between narrow
cracks and crevasses with
mounds of ice-covered snow
peeping out at you!
There is a path; just big enough
for you to pass, leading you
into darkness,
beyond.
Waiting, wanting; needing your
presence to survive.
You are tempted to go but know
not to. You are afraid of what
is lurking in the unknown
emptiness of your soul.

—Kelly Carter

I am waiting,
to see him come winding around the corner,
his hair in the wind,
and his back to the past.
But what if he gets lost,
and goes back to the place he dreads the most,
where he never had any freedom,
but only lots of time on his hands.
Maybe someday he will forget
all the bad times they gave him.
I sure hope he does,
when he finally arrives home.

—Dan Detwiler

THE BACK PORCH

Window sills.
Red flower pots.
Hard dry dirt.
The sun shone down.
Touch,
Hurt,
Don't touch.
Life in a desert
Far away.
Goodbye Grandma.

—Darian K.

AL CAPONE

I'm sitting at the table
in my favorite disco,
drowning my sorrows
with every sip I take from
my Pina Colada.
People are dancing and laughing.
The music vibrates through
my body.
I am so tired of the same
old dull routine,
I want something new and
exciting.
The room becomes filled
with a deep purple mist,
I become dizzy and
out of the corner of my eye
I see this man in a
gray and black pin-striped
suit. He walks up to
me and offers me a
rose.
I look into his deep, menancing
eyes,
sparks fly everywhere.
He pulls me to my feet,
and we go out into
the chill and fog and
noise of Chicago.
Hand in hand,
we cross the street,

but before we reach
his car
a loud thundering noise
reaches my ear
and Al Capone
is lying at my feet
with thick red
blood all over his
gray and black suit.
    I fall to my knees,
and close my eyes
and when I reopen
them, I am still at
my favorite disco, with
the people laughing and the
terrifically loud noise,
and I wonder how
exciting life would be
with Al Capone?

—S.P.

Luz

La luz es brilliante!
Lo ciega todo su vision
Como el tiempos buenos
Ciega el realidad en su vida.
Los arboles hacen sombras en
la tierra
Como impressiones en su vida.
La luz salva las sombras
por siempre.

—Amy Lilly

The light is brilliant!
It blinds all your vision
as the good times
blind the reality in your life.
The trees make shadows on
the land
like impressions on your life.
And the light washes over the shadows
for ever.

—trans. Terry Hermsen

The red sky sillouetted by fleeing
birds
A thunderclap, white lightning

It soars through me
False breezes overcome a defiant withering
leaf
The sun covers its scars with dainty clouds

The air is electric yet static
Contradicting moods surround me

A painting of anger, done in peace
I'm only temporary.

—Nathan Kelly

CHEMISTRY
Odes to the Unknown

The fire is making the water
bubble.
I feed the bubbles for they are
hungry.
They eat and eat until no more can
be put into the hungry water.
The beautiful clear water fogs
to the point it looks white.
The more I feed it the higher the
temperature rises.
Until it can take no more.
There at that point it
must stop.
It is like a web, a fine—lined
web that looks so fragile.
Until someone, who was it,
drops clear water on top of my beautiful
white web of the unknown.

—Kim Clark

Black River Blues

While I was sitting at my desk
trying to write
everyone decided to listen to
hillbilly music.
They must enjoy it,
it drives me crazy.
The poet turned it up as loud
as possible.
The walls started to shake.
The glass started to break.
Mr. Hembree was becoming curious
because the whole school was
curious.
He came to Room 13 with ear plugs
in,
He had grown warts all over his skin.
Mr. Lorinc and the poet got canned
for torture in public school.
When I got out of the mental
institution
3 years later
I lived happily ever after with
4 alligators.

—Laurie

THE '82 YEAR AT B.R.

Way back in 1982
we's low on money and living
off garbage cans too.
The roof caved in and killed 3 or 4,
While the potholes in the driveway
killed 8 or more.
At least one bus would break
down a day leaving 20 kids
stranded on the way.
We got this bright idea to
put up a levy, but people
couldn't afford to buy a Chevy,
So it went defeated down
at the polls, where signs were
hung telling of needed rolls
of toilet paper for the school
bathroom, where 10 a day died
of the fumes.
So Black River High still exists
to this day, despite no money
along the way.
Teach them to decorate the office
we said. The wallpaper fell
and they're all dead.
but the school still runs
unto this day; the lunch room
still serving leftover hay.

—Alice K. Loyd

"NOW WHAT?"

Now that we have been deprived
Now that we are without
Now that they have not wasted
  their money.
What will become of us?

Will we grow narrow
Will we live without thought
We no longer have the right
  to an education
We have to thank the older generation
  for our ignorance

—Anonymous

Mrs. Stinson's Class
Westfield Center Elementary

Proverbs

Skunks are expensive.

—Andy Loudon

When a clock ticks
People tock.

—Jim Lang

STORY OF CHILDHOOD

Running through the
grass,
As if I was being
chased.
Shadows covered
the ground,
A dark one stood out
from others
As I went flying through
the air,
The world turned on its
axis
The sharp pain in my
mouth shattered
my dreams.

—Julie Jackson

THE MYSTERIOUS COOKIE BUYER

Going up to the door
to a lady's house.
I'd feel like a real dummy
if she didn't buy these.

Waiting for her to come
seems like coming to school on
the first day.

Nervous, it seems.
but Anxious it really is.

I knock on the door one more time.
Now I'm feeling like a pessimist.
I never give up.

I start to go away
feeling like a rejected
candybar trying to get sold.
  but not getting sold.

When a nice old lady
comes to the door.
She opens the door
like she thought I was going
to mug her or something.

But she sighs with relief
like a terrible softball player
who catches an easy pop-fly.
I ask her if she would like to buy
some cookies.

She looks the form over
acting like a big professor
grading essay questions.

And now nods her head yes
And she tells me one kind to mark down
  and she tells me her name.
She then pushes me out the door
like she was trying to get rid of me.

I mark it down
As I am thinking it out
Feeling like a detective trying to
figure out a case.

I now realize
that she was
probably missing
her favorite soap opera.

—Caryn Wanko

SONG*

All is quiet this day
I feel like I'm going to freeze
It's getting coldr and coldr
but I'm alive today

But it is over, yes it is
And now I'm going back
To live a long and happy life
Forever and forever!

—Gabe

* This song is about a druid who had to live a year by himself. He sang this song as he was going home on the winter solstice.

VISIT TO THE INSURANCE CO.

The buttons tapping on the computers
  reminds me of the rain.
Their hands moved swiftly
  like a spider after its prey.
The telephones ring like dozens
  of doorbells.
There was a lot of talking
  like a flock of birds.
There was one lady who
  twitched her eyes
 like turning the lights
   on quickly
  and off
    on
    off
    and
    on again.

—Paul Mis

POEM ON POEMS

Poems are gifts from your mind.

Don't barge straight
  into them.
but take your time
and look around the
narrow corners.

There you will find
the gift.
It will be waiting
for you if you give it time.

—Laura Foradori

BOX

Reach inside me
it's an endless tunnel.

Touch me,
I'm waves
constantly rolling across
ths sea,
never stopping to rest.

It reminds me
of a hollow ball,
without bounce,
it lies there
still as a mouse.

I am a hollow whirlwind,
tossing and turning everything
in its path.

A creature lives in me,
like a dragon lives in a cave, and
like people live in houses.

—Cathy Ocheltree

A man sells a hot dog at a hot dog stand
in Washington D.C. while a cow has a calf
at a form by Chippewa Lake. A volcano
erupts in a school cafeteria in New York.
A telephone pole falls down at Yellowstone
Park and a dog barks at a robber in Chicago.

—Annette Palmer

JABBERWOCK

Last night the murderer
got murdered.
I felt
sorang for
him. I first found out
when somebody called
me on my blone.
I was eating my
raver sandwich.
It was a raoudy
day. He said, "I'm
hapsca because
I
just murdered
the murderer!
So I grabbed
my troat,
I ran out
and hopped in my
rodcar and raced
to the house.
It was
smare.
I found
out it
was a fausl.
I was rema.

—Donny Brown

Key:

Sorang = Sorry, angry
Blone = Black phone
Raver = Raw liver
Raoudy = Rainy and cloudy
Hapsca = Happy and scared
Troat = Trench coat
Rodcar = Hotrod car
Smare = Small & red
Fausal = False alarm
Rema = Relieved & mad

LAST WORDS TO THE POET

You made me see
  the world differently
    than I ever have before

To open my eyes
  so I can see the
    the world more clearly

I notice words in songs
  I never have heard before

And now when I look at thistle
  It becomes a popcupine

—Susan Gortner

The winter(tr)ee ice
Stuck to flinging arms flying
And the soundless music stops
When winds unwind.

—Linda Brown
Morton Jr. H.S.
Vandalia

SUNDAY AFTERNOON

Golf is not my game
Keep your head down and your arm straight
Do you like me?
You'll catch on

Keep your head down and your arm straight
Fore!
You'll catch on
Don't hit me with the club

Fore!
You'll hate me before we're through
Don't hit me with the club
Pick up your tee and follow me

You'll hate me before we're through
Pick up your tee and follow me
Golf is not my game
Do you like me?

—Denise Ripp
Smith Jr. H.S.
Vandalia

I AM A LEAF

I dream of myself as a canopy
Protecting a nest that has been
  built and filled with love
I dream of myself as a butterfly
Flying away from this bough
To flit and dip and soar and
Settle upon the sweetest flowers.
I dream of myself as a hydroplane
Settling into the ocean of the cow-pond
  standing at my feet,
Sailing across its vastness
Maneuvering around the stately cattails
  and spread lily pads
I'll take to the sky
Sailing again home to the
Reality of my bough
I dream of myself as a number
Waiting to be chosen
To be taken away on a winter's walk
Only to reappear in a season
With more beauty and purpose.

—Anna Duff
Morton Jr. H.S.
Vandalia

RULES FOR HOMEWORK

1. Complete the homework before the teacher finishes assigning it.
2. Don't do it if you have to open a book.
3. Make up three good excuses for doing the wrong page — just in case.
4. Be sure to put it in your dog's feeding bowl so he'll eat it.
5. Do every other question — the teacher won't know the difference.
6. Fold your paper up and stuff it in your back pocket.
7. Take the wrong book home.
8. Leave the homework on your kitchen table.

—Jana Adams
Morton Jr. H.S.
Vandalia

FUTILITY

Roses, golden, glistening, shining
Pine cones, gold dingle dangle
Ring finger, knuckle to knuckle winking eyes
Hey you got any more jewelry to put on?
Rhinestone shackles glitter, sparkle
silver tic toe displaying tinkle chime
Hey you got any more jewelry to put on?
Shiny gold snake round waist so slim
Pearly twirly pens neatly stuck in
Polished brass buttons.
Piddly, didley pum
Hey you got any more jewelry to put on?

—Vicki Burnett
Southwestern H.S.
Gallia County

PRIDE OR FEAR?

I tossed it out the window
It clung to the sill
Hazing my vision
Defying my will

It clung to the sill
Clouding my vision
Defying my will
It lives with me still

Clouding my vision
Determined in her resolve
It lives with me still
Pride is a fierce contender

Determined in her resolve
Pride is a fierce contender
I tossed it out the window
Hazing my vision.

—Judy Farney
Southwestern H.S.
Gallia County

Moist, woodsy, strangely sweet,
Earthy odours softly creep,
A bird trills hauntingly.

—Mrs. Wilma McCurdy
Holmesville Elementary

Struggle for life, I need the light
Cool rocks become my nemisis
I reach, clinging to cracks
Waiting for new life

Blood begins to flow
Life has begun once again
Hurry — I must hurry
Time is short to renew my grip

—Diane Graebner
Black River H.S.

FATALISM

This is an ode to chaos
a discord of thought and of sound,
Of senses sent reeling,
Of rhyme, reason and feeling
All Jumbled and twisted around.

A million voices are speaking.
A million ears strain to hear.
A flash and a roar,
Dead silence, no more.
A vast sense of darkness and fear.

Strength goes with the feeling of weakness.
Hope crawls through the depths of despair
A pulse of regret
follows all that you get
And uselessness comes after wear.

Light will change into darkness.
Silence replaces the song.
There never was pain
But where joy was the same
And there never was right without wrong.

Genesis marks the beginning
Of this handful of time that is mine.
In exodus fast
Struggle out of the past
To finis, the end of that time.

—Robert Stone
Clay H.S.
(written at about age 18)

WHY?

Life
Each one unique and individual.
Why then are we expected to conform?

Love
Each one a mixture of unexplained emotions.
Why then must we define love?

Experience
Each one based on unknown consequence.
Why then are we expected to choose wisely?

Death
Each an answer to the many myseries of life.
Why then must we die to fully understand?

—C. Parkes
Clay Junior H.S.

THE SEA

The sea calls to me
For we have an affinity,
I am a Cancer and the sea is home.

I love to watch the storms,
The wild, turbulant waves
Pounding against rocky caves,
Showering sprays of glistening droplets.
It excites, yet soothes me, for
This is the majesty, the grandeur, the power of the sea.

I love to walk the quiet beaches
Early in the morning
Drinking the tranquility
Storing up the peace in my soul.

The rhythmic pounding of surf at night
Soothes, lulls and cajoles me to sleep.
I feel secure. I am Cancer. I am home.

—Marge de Sostoa
Librarian
Clay H.S.

ANANSI BALLAD

From Africa, dark and deep,
Comes Anansi in my sleep.

A tale is woven in my mind,
And in my vivid dream I find
Anansi is a wonderous spiderman,
Who is keen of mind and swift of hand.

From where he came, no one knows,
But he has always been, and never grows old.

If Anansi's favor a man has won,
A web he will find that Anansi has spun.

But pity the man upon whom Anansi frowns,
For no happiness for him will ever abound!

But Anansi's magic doesn't stop here;
He's responsible for what the people hold dear.

Traveling silently from plain to plain,
Anansi, it is said, brings on the rain.

He prevents the floods and stops the drought,
And from the huts keeps the tigers out.

With just one look the flowers bloom,
The harvest flourishes, the rivers loom.

My dream takes a turn, and my happy thoughts ebb;
Why couldn't Anansi travel over MY land, spinning his web?

Suddenly my reverie is broken and I awaken.
Was that a noise in the dark, or was I mistaken?

Has my dream gone too far? Where has my imagination led?
A web has been spun over my bed!!!

—Laura Adante
Language Teacher
Hartford Jr. H.S.
Canton

MARGARET HONTON b. 1932
1719 Eddystone Avenue Elem and Sec
Columbus, OH 43224
(614) 263-5168

Margaret earned her BS Ed and MA at the Ohio State University while raising eight children. Since 1975 she has been active in the AIE program. She has published widely as a poet, essayist, critic and editor; her fourth poetry anthology is *I Name Myself Daughter, and It Is Good*. She has published two recent chapbooks in response to photography and painting exhibitions: *Photo-Sensitive* and *Disclosures*. She has a new manuscript on personal dream symbols seeking a publisher.

THE SHADOW

A presence felt, unseen—
The ether mask at Children's Hospital.
The opaque curtain of Limbo
where unbaptized babies go.
Carbon monoxide lingering
over our drowsing family.
Prickles of fiberglas, invisible as the panic
when my brother locked me in the attic.

Sometimes more tangible—
A coal—grimed curtain floating
from a neighbor's upstairs window,
like the voice of a woman pleading,
Let me go, let me go!
The black veil worn by Cat-lick-ers,
those nuns who stalked in pairs to throw
lone children down the sewers.

Sometimes less—
Vapors hovering over the dye vat
where I worked at the knitting mill,
fungus in my bloodstream,
voodoo in my dreams.
A giant Rorschach Test projected
on my nightmares' screen.
A foreboding like the underside
of a star fish not quite dead.

A portent like this moment—
at O'Hare, a jetliner crossing
two hundred feet above
our small plane's taxiing.

Shadow, old Familiar,
you keep me shuddering.

—Margaret Honton

Rubyville Elementary
Scioto County

MY HOMEWORK MAY LOOK MESSY BECAUSE I'M WRITING THIS FROM INSIDE

...an oak tree. I fell in a knothole
and it's stuffy in here.
...a pencil sharpener. The blades
pulled me in.
...a folder. I was putting
some papers in, and I fell in a
pocket. I'm squooshed.
...a basketball. At the place where
you put air in. I was sucked in.
...the refrigerator. I got stuck to
my peanut butter sandwich, and some-
body set me aside for lunch.

—Mrs. Vice's Fourth Grade

MEAN MOUNTAIN

I like to make snow fall.
I block the sun from hitting the town,
and the town is all solar energy.
I'm a magical mountain.
I don't eat, but I blow smoke
and gases and lava and ashes
that cover the town.
and people can't breathe.
I'm the Magical Mountain.
I'm mean.

—Josh Pack
Grade 4

WRITER

I'm a writer. I get ink all over me.
One time I was covered with ink.
and my wife didn't let me in the house.
I slept outdoors almost every night.
A dog came and licked me off, so I went
in the house and she shot me dead.

—David
Mrs. Chandler's 4th grade

WRITER? OR WRAPPER?

Last time I was a wrapper
I wrapped a Christmas present.
Last time I was a writer
I wrote a poem.
But I don't know which I'll be
so now I'll write
and wrap up my will.

—Stephen Foster
Grade 4

IN THE MORNING

In the morning when I woke up I was floating again. I started moving my arms, and flew around the room, so I went to a psychologist and told him my problem. He said I was crazy. Then I popped up out of the chair and began flying. I asked him if he believed me now? He said, "Yes, but there is nothing I can do." So, I went back home and I still float and fly sometimes.

—Harold Hoover
Grade 6

LION'S REVENGE

That lion tamer is asking for it! First he takes me away from my mother, and then he puts me in a cage. Then, after I start to like him, he hits me with a rope and a stick. When he comes in here, I'm going to bite the living daylights out of him. I'm going to hang him by his rope, and put that stick up his nose. Here he comes...

Hey, you lion. You bit me, you monster! Somebody get me a gun, better yet a cannon. Help! Let me out!

—SHOT—

He got out. But I showed him.

—Alvin Bramblette
Grade 6

SCHOOL PICTURE

How neat I look!
I look terrific!
Just absolutely aaaaa.
To cut the short stuff,
I look the best!
That cowboy shirt I had on
didn't do a thing, but
nothing, just nothing
could hide my handsome.

—Jay Niblick
Grade 4

MRS. APART

Hi, I am Mrs. Apart. My friends call me that becaause I am all apart. My hands are hanging in midair, and when I try to walk one foot is above my waist, and I make the wierdest noises tink tank toke, tink tank toke. When they get mad at me they say, "Pull yourself together!" Tink tank toke, tink tank toke...

—Josh Pack
Grade 4

THE VOICE OF EXPERIENCE

I walked around alone, and I saw it, or them. The green giant balls in the sky came down and picked me up. The next thing I knew, I was on another planet where everyone had red hair and wore silvery gym suits, tight to their body. The examined me, and then I was shot with a laxer gun. Half of my body was invisible! Then another shot...I was completely invisible. They returned me to earth, and I was never seen again.

—Shelly Kinker
Grade 6

STOPPING BY WOODS AND GOING ON

Whose woods these are I think I know.
His house is in the village, though;
he will not see me go.
When he comes out
he may shout,
but I'll be gone, and he won't know
Christmas is coming. Ho, Ho, Ho.

—Shawn Bare
Grade 6

ALONE

It's fun to be alone
up here on the hill.

You can see the sunset
and the town below is still.

The weather is nice:
I'm away from the crowds.

It's just the right climate
To picture koalas in the clouds

People don't know what it's like,
How pleasant being all alone.

But there is one problem,
There's no TELEPHONE.

—Becky Lewis
Grade 5

DREAM SHARING

I was back in the old days. I was an old man, and there in an old dusty room were big boxes you could go through. You could open a big cement door, move a mean dog, and go in. I was a king thrown into a tank of black pirranhas. I was in my suit of armor, so I sank very fast. I drew my sword and killed every last pirranha. Then I went up for air, and something grabbed me —something with one eye and a mouth with blood soon to be my blood. Now I remember, silver bullets can kill him...

—Miss Staten's 5th grade

MY HEAD IS A MESS

I need my hair cut
My moustache itches
My eyes are blue
My brain isn't fastened
I can not think
My ears are dirty
I've got to feed my face

—Daria
Grade 5

DREAMS OF THE ANIMALS

Animals dream about getting smashed
or shot. They think people have
iron in their backbone.

A cat has a nightmare about getting
hit on the head with a broom. It
dreams of having a whole gallon of
milk.

A deer dreams that the mountain lion
that's chasing him falls off a cliff.

A German shepherd has a nightmare
about an iron cage and metal chains.

A white mustang has a nightmare
about having a bit in its mouth.

A 6-foot rabbit dreams about a new
hat and coat and pair of jeans.

A teenage monkey named Shelly dreams
of love. When she sees Mikey, the
boy of her dreams, she goes crazy
over him.

—Mr. Pack's 4th grade

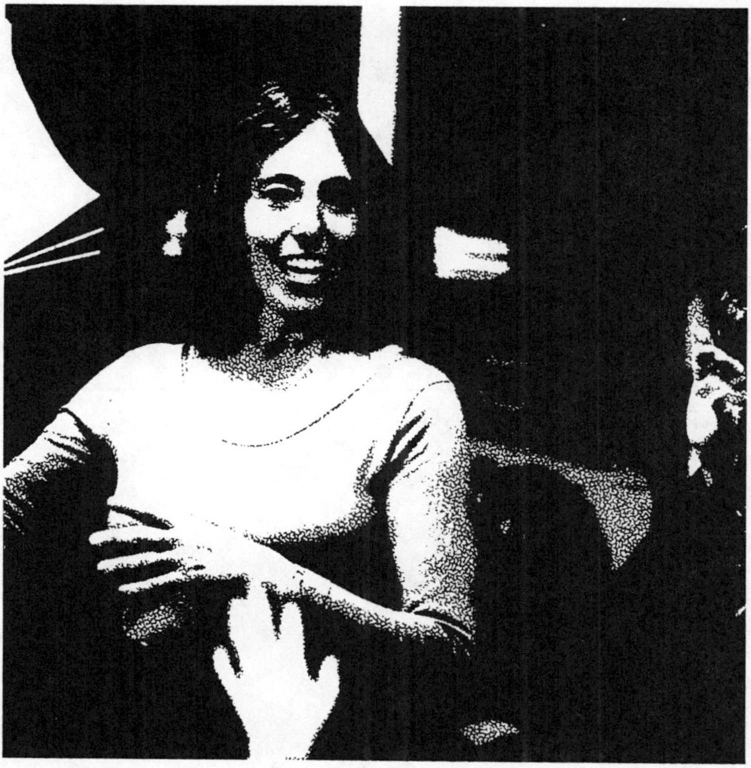

ELEANOR KEATS b. 1930
9261 E. Berry Avenue
Englewood, CO 80110
(303) 779-1297

Eleanor was born in New York City and educated at Cornell, the University of Denver, and Juilliard in addition to several of Europe's fine music schools. She has read widely on radio and TV in the Pacific Northwest, midwest and southwest. Her multi-media works, involving poetry, music, slides and film, have been presented in England and Paris as well as in the United States. Her poems have appeared in many magazines in this country and abroad, including the ANTIOCH REVIEW, the HUMANIST, and the BLOOMSBURY REVIEW. Last year she was a winner in Denver's Bonfils Theatre competition, resulting in an evening's poetry performance there, with an avante-garde percussionist.

POEMS FOR SINGING

1

We are the eyes
  of the sun
we set everything
  afire
when our skin
  melts away
we are singing birds

2

We are the eyes
  of wells
we can talk
till the end
  of echoes
if a stone
  is thrown in
  to vibrate
  our waters
we are a singing
  stone

3

We are the eyes
of vibraphones
we sound on and on
our pipes are long roots
that sing our glitter
and our descending
   agony
we cascade together
with one swoop
of the stick

though our bodies
  are brittle
and may break any second
in the sea of sound

4

We are the eyes
  of silence
nothing needs to sound
when the eyes fuse
and the heartbeat
  continues
its warm, constant
  ticking

5

We are the eyes
that need bodies
to enter the dark,
the dark
that warms our skin
that has fallen away,
the dark
that weaves bodies
  together
to keep the light
from falling out
of the eyes

Eleanor Keats

Morton Jr. H.S.
Smith Jr. H.S.
Vandalia 1981

Collage Poems

Victory alas
Girls in Las Vegas
Drinking liquor not too smartly
It is a miracle
her eyes are easy
Magically something fell from the sky.

—Todd Stevens

Jogging the wind going
through your hair,
boxing the pounding
hitting your face
chicken the
crunching
sound and
the feeling
lips the touching
of two people's lips.

—Tom Blakely

Kathy's fringes are like the horse's
mane her beauty is like the horse's fur,

Linda's hair is like a peacock
while the water falls like snow
around her in the pool,

Tammy's hair is like the golden
sunlight from the window glass
her face is as smooth as the sheets
she lays on,

Tina's teeth are as bright as her
diamonds on her dress her hair
matches her eyes.

—Rick McBride

People

Somehow I envy them
The people who are famous.
Giving their fake smiles for the camera.
The cat has his milk.
Clothes of many colors
Attract your attention,
Rock stars keep playing the music I love.
The poems I read
Help me see what's inside.

—Sharon Simpson

The hunter gets a caribou
like a president gets a car.
Boats go to water,
and I have a guitar.
I want to go to the Bahamas,
but it's so far.
Jelly fills my belly
like a boat will float.
Crocodiles gather in piles for miles.
A crab reminds me of a sister.

—Chuck Hill

MOTORCROSS

You sump on your dirt bike and start
It up and you hear the roar of your cycle
Then you give it some gas switch
gears and you're off around the track
and you hear all the other cycles roaring
and screaming and you pull the throttle
all the way back and you listen to
your own motorcycle roar and
scream and all the excitement comes
out of going fast across the dirt and
over the hills flying through the air.

—Dave Murphy

COLD FIELD

The fog lies still as if it were dead,
big iron gates lay on the dead field,
instead of seeds, there are stones
cold stones of has-beens
mothers fathers brothers sisters
what once was memories good and bad
lie under those stones, not people
just memories

—Kelly Vogler

FROZEN MORNING

A frozen chilled
Morning
With no one wanting
To leave their beds
The store windows
With bright white designs
The locks
Frozen
Shut

—Tarsha Billingcoe

Snow is like a flock of doves
flying south.
Snow is like a bag full of diamonds
crushed.
Snow is like the dew that lies
across the meadow.

—Lisa Lockhart

I remember one night
I was lying in my bed
thinking out of nowhere,
I was thinking of
so many things it
was like being in another
world; I felt like I was
in fire, and then in ice.
My bed felt like water
on clouds. Then I looked
out of my window and
the moon glared in and
shown up my whole room.
It looked like it had
diamonds all over it with
crystals too. Then a little
bit later, the stars were
filling the sky with
happiness and I
slowly fell asleep
with the moon and
stars showing on my face.

—Stacey Rodgers

Remembering

The lightning hit,
the thunder booming
like horses hoofs running
in the night.
The fire shooting,
shooting like a falling star. Outside
the rain was sildly hitting
the rooftops. It was drowning
the poor innocent flowers.
The tree limbs were being thrown about
hitting each other violently.
Inside the house
I sit watching the amazement
of nature. Then the piece of wall
falls, sounding like a mountain
falling down. I was grabbed and
pulled into my neighbor's house,
where they opened their arms and
welcomed us.

—Angie Daugherty

The icicles hang there,
silently
Like the mouth of the winter
giant.
But soon his teeth start to
melt away.
The giant grows old
As young winds turn
him into a toothless spring.

—Cathy Ratcliff

SKY POEM

When my brother died,
the sky turned darker,
The clouds were like a
cover over him, and the
expression on his face
was showing, it was so
clear, the flowers I put
on his grave were there,
I could see them, I
pushed away some of his
blanket, behind it was his
grave, I broke down in tears.

—Jenny Elliott

My room is like wild
animals in the wilderness,
tropies hanging on the
wall, as if they're alive

My bow sitting on the
feet ready to shoot another one.

Arrows sharp as a bear tooth,
the deer fur on the wall crawling
up the wall like a snake
could crawl in grass

trophies on my shelves
sitting there shining and bright,

my drapes are
like the woods, my wall
is like the wild animals.

—Mark Pooler

My room is like a moving truck
with all the furniture packed way back
into every corner.
A boy stands in it wondering what to do.
He decides to lie down on a board
and lifts something for exercise.
The sun beats down on the old rug,
the boy leaves, and the room has no life once again.

—Scooter Smith

ODE TO SPRING

And in come the warm winds
they push away the hands that hold
the earth in a cold freeze
they bring with them life
the life of the once frozen world
and out come the flowers from their
warm earthen homes
they burst forth with an array of
colors more brilliant than the rainbow
and then the trees bud
their buds soon blossom into
beautiful, full leaves
they protect the earth from the
new hot sun
and now the brooks flow
their currents bring on life
the life of the frogs, and the turtles
and the animals that live in its midst
so spring is joy
the joy of a new tomorrow
the joy of a new found life.

—Melissa Banks

Science fiction is cool, it
Is entertaining as well as
Imaginative. Then there's soap
Operas. You can see a soap opera
Once a year and still keep up
With the story. Soap operas
Can brainwash a housewife
In a week. The only thing
They're good for is to have a
Conversation between two old
Biddies who have nothing else
To do but gossip and burn
Dinner.

—David Hellard

Dream Poems To Music (Pachelbel's Canon)

THE UNICORN

The unicorn stands silently
Watching the dove
It falls, and rises up again
All in one movement
Circling the sky.
The clouds,
Clouds softly rolling,
to cover the sky,
turning from white, to gray, black
The first drop of rain falls,
rolling down the unicorn's horn
and onto his back, falling silently.

—Susan Graham

His eyes were drunk,
All glazed over as though
He had been invaded

She had eyes that were searching.
They were trying to see through
The blackness of the deep water.
But there was nothing.

Nothing but the two glowing eyes
That shone faintly as though dead.
They were the drunken eyes that she saw.
But, she couldn't move, the eyes were
closer.

—Lori Leach

"Go Away" Poems

Go away, he said
shouting like a lion
would roar,
    Go away now,
then he ran out of the house,
running like a horse.

Go away, he shouted,
running down the valley
chasing the boy.

The moon rises silently,
like a grasshopper whispering,
  jumping around the world,
  and when the grasshopper
    sleeps
the moon will go away
like the stars too.

—Mark Pooler

Go away, he said
stepping out of the room,
for the night is still and the moon
rises silently like a snake slithering
through the grass, for I want to be alone
like one star in the day.

—Robbi Fulton

Come here I said in a soft
voice like a clock's tick.
Stepping into the room.
It was getting dark, the
moon was starting to rise.

As I started to get in bed
I suddenly felt like a deer
hopping in the woods
finding a comfortable spot
then I started to doze off.

—Angie Crawford

WATER

Moving swiftly like
a runner in a race
moving
along a road of rocks

—Bev Taylor

The sycamore tree
reaching into the sky
at night
roaming in the wind

—Bruce Whisman

FORGOTTEN

Dangling from the ceiling
Like a Trapeze
Without an artist
Tangled and useless,
Left alone, forgotten.
Not of use for anyone
Soon to be captured
By a yellow straw broom.
Unneeded and unnoticed,
Grayed with dust
Still until a breeze,
No one remembers
The web

—Susan Graham

TORNADO

The tornado shrieked like a terrible freight
train, tearing through towns,
twirling and spinning
like a top that wouldn't stop,
shaking the houses until they collapsed,
rattling and tattering everything in its path,
slapping and hitting the fresh green grass,
a gray-black tunnel
roaring through the breeze,
twisting and torturing
the great tall trees,
three scared kids
caught in the bathtub,
door spread over them like a coffin,
branches driven through telephone poles,
terrified people running through the town.

7th grade

Holmesville Elementary School

A POEM ABOUT RAIN

If there would be no rain
Nothing would grow in the ground
If there would be no rain
Trees and plants would not grow
But one thing that I like
Is that I can splash in the puddles
And I play in the rain.

—Ryan Hostetler
Grade 2

LIGHT

When the light comes over the valley
I sit and watch.
It makes me feel like a soaring bird
So free in the air.
When the light is gone
Every thing is so dark and peaceful.

—Todd Summers
Grade 4

A butterfly fluttered
As it landed on a flower.
And now a bud fell from the rose.

—Merci Schlegel
Grade 3

The flower was blowing in the wind.
The sky was blue as a diamond,
The field was wandering with the wind.

—Renee Ryneer
Grade 6

My first time riding a horse
Dad smoking a cigarette
Pulling the reins,
The horse jumpy.
I hang on hang on,
Dad drops the cigarette
The horse takes off running
with the wind.
I fall off,
the wind stops.

—Christie Humrichouser
Grade 5

I am floating down the stream
I am a frog
And fish shiny like gold
And the water is making shadows
The sun is shining down
From the sky
On the earth
And the birds in the trees
Along the streams
Are singing a soft little song.
The tall weeds aong the little stream
Are blowing softly.

—Mae Miller
Grade 6

LIGHT

The
light
there
is
no
light
it
is
cold
the
bears
are
sleeping
the
rabbits
are
nibbling
at
stems
of
carrots
my
brain
is
ticking
away
Birds
are
in
my
head
butterflies
in
my
stomach
snakes
in
my
arms
yes!

I
see
it
now
spring
is
coming
I
hear
the
birds
chirping
way
the
pond
is
not
frozen
anymore
the
children
are
starting
to
feed
squirrels
peanuts
again
the
sun
trying
to
escape
the
snow
clouds
yes
spring
is
here

at
last

—Tammy Hostettler
Grade 5

THE SUN

The day begins like a turtle
The sun rises slowly
In the breeze of the wind.

Crows are beginning to wake up
They make beautiful sounds,
In the misty rays of the sun.

The trees whisper
Like corn fields
in the wind of the morning.

The sun is very bright
in the season of summer
the winds chant like a clock.

—Dennis Troyer
Grade 6

THE BLUE BIRDS

They sound like the wind
Going through the grass
They glide on air,
Like the clouds.
They are free in the air
So like the wind.
So like the blue sky.

—Geneva Beachy
Grade 4

DIANE KENDIG
3117 East Derbyshire
Cleveland Heights, OH 44118
(216) 932-0647

Elem and Sec

Diane is a native of Canton and began writing at age 10. She attended Otterbein College as an undergraduate and after teaching high school Spanish and English for four years, she moved to Cleveland and received an MA from Cleveland State University. In addition to publishing in many periodicals and anthologies, a collection of her work, *A Tunnel of Flute Song,* was published by the Cleveland State University Press in 1980. She also has a prose selection in *Ariadne's Thread: Contemporary Women's Journals* (Harper and Row, 1982)

WRITING IN A SONNET

"A sonnet is a steamy place where a lot
of people go to sweat."

a fourth grader

At first you'll fight this space and long for flight.
Think: others stayed without suffocation.
Here air's rarefied. And don't imagine
the door is your way out. Instead, sit tight and look for
subjects. Note that there are none
but two too risky: breathlessness and white.
Once used to them, use things that flow just right:
your sweat, for one, will have fruition soon.
Now see how much this takes of you and write.
Write your nakedness and perspiration,
nobel elements of emulation,
your fingers shrunk to wattles, your head light.
Before you're all wrung out, don't lose what lured
you here, and find a decent rhyming word.

—Diane Kendig

IN THE DAY WHEN WE CAN'T SEE THE STARS....

They disappear from us.
High in the sky, they sleep, they hide.
They make a big ball by gathering up:
  Round different bright colors. Big white
    and yellow lights.
  The ball comes apart.

They eat clouds for breakfast:
  white and blue, sweet and storm clouds.
They drink sun and rain and snow and sweat.

They don't go to school. They go to a place,
  The Black Hole by the moon
  where there are white and gray clouds
  and it's heavenly.
They play games like
Run Around Saturn, Kick the Moon, Duck, Stars;
  Ring Around Saturn, Run around Heaven,
  Star in the dell, and Leap Stars.

They zigzag.
They have babies called babystars; they're small and
    have less light.
They say, "good morning," "goodnight," and
  "dark, dark, dark, dark."

They look out the windows and look at their clocks.
It gets dark and cold. They see the moon.
It is time.

They light up.

—Mrs. Flag's First Grade Class

NIGHT SCHOOL

The whole school turns upside down.
The stage breaks out in creepy things: spiders, tarantulas.
The flag pledges itself.
The books read themselves and tear each others' pages.
The curtains turn into ghosts who type on the typewriters.
The chalkboard turns to grass.
All the pictures come down off the walls:
  Our bunny goes in every class and scribbles on
    teachers' papers.
  The rest of the pictures dance
  As the record player sings a ghostly song into the loud-
speaker.
Numbers come down and count themselves.
Desks come alive and play school:
  They eat crayons and chalk for lunch
  And eat glue.
The bell comes down into the school and paints a face
    on itself,
In Mrs. Zimbello's class, the floor turns to water and
    the paper fish swim.
That's why, when we come to school this morning, our
  classroom was wet.

—Mrs. Zimbello's First Grade Class

SOUR SEA MONSTERS

Sour sea monsters stink.
Anybody knows that sour sea monsters stink.
Aunt Oty has a sour sea monster.
Nobody else has a sour sea monster.

—Sean Hayes
Grade 2

TIME FOR A FROGASTORY

Once a frog and a toad were listening to a tale. "And beware of the Icepoo! And beware of the Icepoo!" said Toad. He turned around and Said, "There's the Icepoo!" Frog was laughing and toad was looking at a story book.

—Paul Moore
Grade 3

ODE TO THE SPACE SHUTTLE

Space shuttle, Hurry up!
Get repaired and launched.
If you have to, launch yourself
and leave the astronauts behind.
Go explore the universe all by yourself.
You'll have lots of fun
picking up rockets and satellites.

—Greg Ellis
Grade 3

ODE TO GUINEAPIG

You fuzzy silly thing.
You like to squeak and eat.

You kick all the wood chips
out of your cage.

You like to chew
on Mom's plants, you silly thing.

You like to crawl up
on my shoulder.

I like you because you're funny
and do silly things.

—Sue
Grade 3

ODE TO THE DRESSER

You hold my clothes.
You're white with gold stripes.
You're square with nine drawers.
Sometimes you hold my books.
I'm glad the dresser was invited.

—Becky Witt
Grade 3

SPAGHETTI, SPAGHETTI, DELICIOUS SPAGHETTI

Little meatballs, oh, so delicious.
Like little red balls
going down your throat.
The long strings of noodles:
Yum! Yum!

Down! Down goes the spaghetti.
Oh! so hot!
It burns my mouth.
Ouch!
It burned my mouth.

—Betsy Guthrie
Grade 3

I PRAISE EYES

Eyes help me see.
They would look like clouds in the sky.
What is it like to have eyes?
What makes eyes unhappy?

—Shawn Wagner
Grade 3

SHE STILL TALKS ABOUT HIM or GOOD-BYE, YOUNG ONE

You know it's really hard
when you lose someone or something.
I know how it feels.
I have an aunt,
She had a baby,
but she never got to see it
because it died
when it was born.

And yet, she still talks about him,
and it doesn't bother her,
so she must have got used to it.

Good-bye, Young One, Good-bye.

—Heather M.
Grade 3

GRANDPAW AND GRANDMAW

Wmen my grandpaw used to be living, he used to rock us in his favorite rocking chair. I still remember that chair, that chair, that chair. I liked when he rocked us, too. My grandmaw died, too, and I was very sad. I loved them a lot and even though they died, I still love them both. And I know where their grave is.

—Brian Ries
Grade 3

MY DOG DIED

My dog died.
I don't know why
He died.
He got shot.
That's *how* he died.

My dad cried
when my dog died.
He died.

—Anonymous
Grade 3

SNEAKER

Oh, sneaker, oh, sneaker.
I like you, sneaker.
You make me run fast, faster,
than anyone else.
I like you, sneaker.

—David Norman
Grade 3

AN ODE TO THE WORLD

World, I am glad you are here.
If you were not, I would not be here.
You're a beautiful green & mostly blue.
From far away you just look like a thing.
But I know that is no trouble.
I know people say
you will come to an end, but I know
  that's not true.
You will always be here to guide me through

—Rebecaa Ausprung
Grade 3

THE WILD HORSES

It almost seems like
They fly around on the air.
It looks very beautiful.

—April Vaugn
Grade 4

THE NIGHT

The night is so dark.
No light no sounds.
Because everybody is asleep
at night. The stars are so
dense and shiney.

—Ben Berry
Grade 4

JAMES C. KILGORE
Cuyahoga Community College
Eastern Campus
4520 Richmond Road
Warrensville Township, OH 44122
(216) 464-1450 (W)
(216) 292-6730

Born in Louisiana, Jim has degrees from Wiley College and the University of Missouri. Currently, he is a professor of English at the Cuyahoga Community College in Cleveland. He is a veteran of military service with the Army in Italy, Austria and Germany during the second world war, and has read his poetry at colleges and universities across the country. His poems, essays and stories have appeared in such periodicals as BLACK WORLD, PHYLON, PRAIRIE SCHOONER and OBSIDIAN; his eighth volume, *African Violet: Poem for a Black Woman* was published in 1982. Also in 1982, the Ohio Poetry Day Association chose him as Ohio Poet of the Year.

UNTIL I MET YOU

Until I met you
I wanted to watch Hawaiian women
  dancing to sea wind and ukelele music;
I want to see sensuous red California suns
  bow in silky splendor
  before pastel pacific characters.
I wanted to dance to Nigerian drums,
To feast on the luscious grapes of France,
To drink coconut wine in Ghana,
To pray in the temples of Jerusalem:
I dreamed of the glories of exotic and holy
  places,
Until I met you.

—James C. Kilgore
From *African Violet: Poem for a Black Woman*
published by Lotus Press

WHY COULDN'T THEY HELP YOU?

I hear your voice crying out for help.
I see you falling upon your knees
I didn't notice the call of death was upon you.
Why couldn't they help you?
I know I was small and fairly young, but
I remember your joyous smile and vibrant kiss.
I also remember your smooth skin and soft touch.
Why couldn't they help you?
I smell your cologne, although you are gone.
I dream of you day in and out
I wish you were here without a doubt
I can't forget the day I cried out for you.
As I watched those mean men come carry you threw.
I do want to forget the day mommy said
"Honey please understand but
Daddy is dead."

—Tanya Bass

BLUES

The blues are like an old weeping
willow tree.
They hand their branches real low all
over me.
And on a sunny day when I think
it's about to fade.
It covers me o'er again providing
unwanted shade.
At night it seems to softly whisper
tearing me apart.

—Debra Gipson

WHY DID IT HAVE TO BE YOU?

Leaving others in grief
We remember the pains in your heart
Your tears were overflowing.

Someone up above heard your cries
He thought for a while,
Then he reached his hand out of the skies
To wipe away your tears.

It was then that he decided
That your soul and body were tired,
He took you in his arms
And rocked you slowly to sleep.

We will always remember you
With the warmest thoughts,
Tears may well up in our eyes
But that's how it is when one dies.

—Zelda Martin

Shaker Heights High School

GHAR DALAM

You walk along a foggy street
lit only by streetlights
which gives the fog a
luminescence of its own and
in your mind is the ringing
of two strange words
Ghar Dalam
suddenly you are transported
to the highest mountain on a small island
looking down on your castle of marble
with a dome of gold which
shines as brightly as the setting sun

you reflect on the craftsmanship of
your ancestors who built the castle
untold centuries ago
you look upon the cove
and see the fishermen returning to the village
you smile with pride over the island
you rule and
say its glorious name
GHAR Dalam
you find yourself on the same
road wondering what your vision signified
and the two strange words
Ghar Dalam
you are then aboard a galley as a slave
forced to row your lord's ship
your back aches with the whippings
the slavemaster gives you for
not keeping up with the rest and
you feel both hunger and thirst
you look up at your lord who strangely
resembles yourself
you look at him with pain and scorn
but he only ignores you
you grow angry at the idea that if you
had simply been born in the right cradle
you could have been the lord of the
island whose name burns you like fire
and takes a place in your mind like a curse
Ghar Dalam
you quietly find that the ship and the
island are only parts of a strange image as you
come back to the road
a kind of dream from the back corner of your mind
a light rain starts to fall
but you don't mind
yet you still hear the two words
shouting from within your mind
Ghar Dalam

—Joseph Love

QUERIDA ADRIANA

Can you see within
yourself?
do you know the
pain inside me
when I see pain
in your eyes of
porcelain blue?
must we hurt
each other when
we know that
the hurt reflects
back like light in a
mirror?
we look at each other
with our eyes but
never with our
hearts
we speak with
our mouths but
never with our
souls
and if our souls
would speak
what words of love
would pass between them!
let us free ourselves
from the outside tyranny
and see ourselves as we
truly are
Canst thou see within
thyself?

—Joseph Love

THE FERRIS WHEEL

Fleeing inward to get out
Turning outward to get in
without peace in time.
On the Ferris Wheel
...now off.

—Cindy Challenger

TO A POET
—for Sylvia Plath

To a poet, any poet:
You sing a song,
But no-one understands the words.

To a poet, any poet:
You flaunt.
With your eyes closed, do not expect to see
inside 'my' world.

To a poet, any poet:
You fall tender to any fetish gloat.
And without a thought, find yourself hung
in hell without a prize.

—Gail Atherly

NEAR A CREEK'S FALL

Here in this land where the brine surfs
on a floor of moving fall, the troubles of
the mind are temporarily washed clean just
as the fall cleanses the face of the slate
it spills over.
Here the noiseless noise of the fall
brings forth dreams of happiness and
thoughts profound.

—Arnelle Moore

A communication is a parasite
that lives off of another, larger animal
called a trust.
A trust is a nearly extincted animal
of the human trait species.
When all of the trusts have died,
the communication will have died as well.

—Arnelle Moore

ZENA KRALL
3544 Fairmount Blvd.
Shaker Heights, OH 44118
(216) 932-1547

Elem and Sec

Zena has a BA in English from the State University of New York at Buffalo, an MA in English from Case Western Reserve University, and is currently attending the Cleveland Institute of Art. She has published poetry in literary magazines in this country and abroad, taught composition in community college, raised three children, read her poetry in a junkyard, and is currently crocheting art sweaters.

WHY THE FIRST SNOW FINDS US WEARY

Each season adds its own load to the weariness
the strain of spring mud and running sap
pricked by the witches' brew of greening shoots,
until we find ourselves counting
babies born in the tops of trees, in underground tunnels,
they make us hear each heaving breath
each sounding under the pillows of our neighbors
until we carry armloads of blossoms
and stow them in the baggage of our dreams
until we wake up with insects dancing in our hair
and lose the earth that cakes beneath our feet
we melt into the summer heat
the rainbows settle, blazing on our skin
until nothing can remove the haze from our eyes
water becomes a mere memory of water
bright fall settles into a worry of brown
dried as old leaves casting spells
until there is nothing but these desperate maps
these naked heavy trees
we beg until they are corpses covered with snow
by those falling angels that crown our weariness white

—Zena Krall

Originally appeared in THE AKROS REVIEW, Number 4

Shreve Elementary School

Fantastic House Poems
Fourth Grade

A MOUSE LIVES IN MY HOUSE

My house is made of
cans, and fish, and eyes
and cars and fish skin.

—Nyla Rogers

GONE HOUSE

The house I made was made of
cans and bottles.
It took me twelve years
to get enough cans and bottles
to make it.
After I made it,
I made a house out of
paper, a big wind came and blew them away.

—Anonymous

BOOK HOUSE

My house is made out of books.
I read every book.
But only one a day!
I wrote most of them.
I add one a day to my house
My books are all different shapes!

—Niki

I made my house out of different things.
A little elevator made of gold
Takes me from room to room.
My house is red, my roof is gold.
Three statues of button cats stand in front.
My bed is made of wood with a centipede on top.
A garden of flowers stands in front.
I got my stuff from a peddler man
Walking aside the road.
It took five years to build.

—Angela Bebb

MY FISH HOUSE

My fish house is shaped like a fish.
It's green and white.
It has 20,000 fins.
It is in New Mexico.
It has a fish kitchen,
a fish couch, and three rooms.

—Jeff F.

MY CARD HOUSE

I made my house
out of cards. It took
me two years to build my house.
I used a jack of hearts,
a queen of spades, a king of
diamonds, and an ace of clubs.
My house is in Florida.
It is as purple as a grape.
It is as big as king kong.
It has eleven rooms, ten doors,
and floors.
It is shaped like a person.
It has shiny walls and ceilings.
My house is red as a rose.
It has thirty windows.

—Marsha P.

My house is very strange,
it is made out of steel & wood.
It is a pig with eyes for windows.
Its tongue went out for a slide.
That is all I can remember
So that's all I can tell you
Except that his foot was a door
And the furniture was made of cotton.

—Marci Hodge

I had a house, it was underground.
It was six feet deep!!!
Twenty thousand feet long,
Sixteen feet high!!!
My furniture is made out of dirt.

—Anonymous

My house is made out
of bones from animals.
My house is 100 years ole.
And it looks like a rock.
The rock is as big as a mountain.
The colors are blue and red.
The face is pretty.

—Becky G.

I made a house out of paper wads.
I made a house that took me two years.
I made a house that looks bright as a rainbow.

—Anonymous

MY BANANA HOUSE

My banana house is big,
It is like a half of moon,
It has one door made of little bananas,
it also has six windows, a banana chimney.
My furniture is made of bananas.

—Michelle Manson

My house has four floors
and six doors.

It has twenty windows
and twenty windowpanes.
It looks like a sandcastle,
washing away.

It has sculptures all around...
And the king and queen live there,
and the queen has long hair.

—Anonymous

My house is made out of ice.
It took me two years to make it.
My house is white.
It took five hundred chips of ice.
It's a hundred feet wide and
a hundred feet tall.
It has two tiger faces carved in it.
It's in Antartica.
It cost a million dollars but
if my girlfirend buys it
then it costs only a dime.

—Anonymous

MY HIDE OUT

Mr. Bones come come to my hide out.
It is in the mountains on a cliff.
Come, come to Dracula and Bones house.

—Anonymous

TREE PLACE

My secret place is in a tree.
I knock three times and it appears.
I pass a dragon and I pass dwarfs.
I fall into a hole and there I am.
jmy furniture is bright with gold.

—Peter Schlamo

Fifth Grade Creation Poems

STARS

Thre Great Creator took raindrops and blew them up, and made many thousands, and he placed them in the sky as stars.

—Ethan

FLOWERS

The flowers were made by Rain Bows. One day a Rain Bow fell from the sky! All the colors flew off the rain bow and on the flowers, at that time the flowers didn't have colors.

—Sharon Miller

THE MAKING OF THE EARTH

After 100 years God was scanning the galaxy.
He noticed that the firebird put the sun up
freezing planets. After that he saw one planet
was perfect. He looked down there.
He ordered an angel to scan the planet.
The angel saw nothing but rocks so he told
God that there was just rocks and mud
and dirt. So God made the dinosaurs, stars,
monsters. —Chad Miles

SLEEPY KING

A sleepy King went
to the pizza parlor
and forgot
where his castle was
and he thought he saw
his castle but it was where
his dragon lived.
And his dragon cooked him
for breakfast.

—Anonymous

SPACE

Pigs in space eating the lace
of space.

—Andy Troutman

Fourth Grade Poems
with Spanish words

ROJO ISLAND

Once there was a rojo island.
Everything was rojo.
Flowers were rojo.
The house was even rojo.
Curtains were rojo.
the grass and trees were rojo.
Until...
A verde monster came.
He painted everything green.

—Marsha Purvis

THE OTHER SIDE OF THE MOON

The other side of the moon
is azule, rojo, and muchos other colores
On the other side of the moon
there are gatitos and caballos and elephantes.
The celo is brun and gris and has montanas.

—Hal

THE PLATA LUNA

The plata luna
shines on the mar.
The plata luna
shines on me.
So pretty and pale.
The plata luna shines
on the caballo standing
next to me.
The plata luna shines
on a blanco blanket
of snow
next to me.

—Julie Gray

THE CABALLO

The caballo is brun.
It is very pretty.
He eats verde grass.
He likes to walk by luna light.
And at day I ride him at dawn.
I love to look at the azule celo.
It is very pretty.

—Melly Tate

Fantasies and Quiet Poems
By Fourth Graders

FUNERAL

The people stood on the grass
Some wore black suits
Some wore black dresses
Some drove in a car
Some walked there
Some trees stood on green grass.
Some have white houses.
Some have black cars.
Some black people have died.
Some white people have died.
Some people have come to the funeral.
Some people have come to be
nice and helpful.

—Todd Young

Come With Me Poems After Walt Whitman
Fifth Grade

Come with me to see the beautiful cloud
It has flowers like roses.

—Roger

I know something that you con't
I can go anywhere!
I can take you!
We could go to a different universe!
Inside an ant hill!
And the most secret place of all!
The room is the center of the earth!

—Ethan

Come with me,
You'll learn a secret about flowers.
Come with me,
I'll tell you something that no one else knows.
Not the farm animals, wild animals,
Or any human being knows this secret.
So come with me and you will see,
What I have to tell.
Roses, violets, hollyhocks, lilys.
I'll tell you about their seeds.
Daffodils, carnations, sunflowers,
You'll hear about their petals.
Come with me and, "Oh,"
Learn a secret.

—Deanna Alcorn

My little puppy and I shall show you
A place where you may have all the food you want
And where no fleas, no one, nobody
Can hurt you or bother you.
But you must promise not to tell anyone
It's a secret between you and me!

—Bobbi Kaufman

Come with me and let's go see the world
You must not tell anybody
You and I will vanish into nowhere.

—Anissa Harmon

WHAT RAIN SAYS

It says come with me
to the center of the earth
Come with me to the inside of the mud
come with me, we'll soar to the clouds
Or the inskirts of the earth
just come.

—Steve

Come with me my friend
and we shall see the birds
high in the sky
and the water singing
the grass talking
come with me.

—Tim

WHAT A RIVER SAYS

I'll show you beauty
I'll show you crawdads, fish anything
I'll show you people
Just come with me

—Steve

WHAT GRASS TELLS YOU

I'll tell you where the frogs jump
  I'll tell you where the worms are
I'll tell you, just come let me tell you.

—Steve

COME WITH ME...
To an inside of a hog.
See the blood freshly flowing.
See the heart pumping blood.
See how the hog moves.
See the brain working.
See the breathing of it.

—Scott Flinner

"In My Mind" Poems
Fourth Grade

MY CONVERSATION WITH MY VOICE BOX

Sometimes I wonder why I talk.
One crazy lazy afternoon the sun was shining in
  my eyes.
I was reading a book and I looked all around.
The sound seemed to be coming from my neck.
When I saw nothing I said, "Oh heck I've been
    reading too much."
Then I heard it again. I couldn't believe my ears.

—Vic

WINTER WITH MY FEET

You go walking in the winter snow
and your toes fall off. The next day
you go walking in the snow and your
feet fall off. And all the time you go
you fall apart. Then you are gone.

—Chuck Conway

ONCE I HAD A BRAEGHT

It was magic. I could fly.
It was sort of yellow and dark bown.
I named it Braety. He was only
fifteen years old. At least that's what
his planet thinks. Of course, they count
by fives. He takes me on lots of rides
on his magic carpet. He could turn people
into dogs. The dogs are smarter and people
would bark and crawl. He could make animals
different colors and striped.

—Melanie Tate

SILENT THINGS

In the spring, our old oak tree in bloom
Next to my black pony in the meadow
On the ledge in the forest path my dad made

A racoon catching fish and washing them
A gentle stream
Rabbits when they eat
A fawn drinking
Anew born calf sleeping

—Mrs. Morris' Fourth Grade Class

DEVON McNAMARA
Box 296
Philippi, WV 26416
(304) 739-2471

Devon has degrees from New York University and the University of Illinois. Since 1976 she has been a resident poet in five states, working with a variety of age groups in public schools, summer camps, a girls' correctional facility, programs for the gifted and special ed., adult summer sessions, and colleges. While an associate professor at Alderson-Broaddus College she launched a radio series "Women and Literature" for West Virginia Public Radio. Her poems have appeared in such periodicals as DARK HORSE, THE HIRAM POETRY REVIEW, THE LAUREL REVIEW, and TRELLIS; she is a contributor to the interview series "Artists and Their Inspiration" for THE CHRISTIAN SCIENCE MONITOR, and she is working on a forthcoming collection of poems, *Driving*.

THAT GREEN FUSE

For Naomi Suconick Myrvaagnes
Because the proper response to poetry is
Not criticism
But poetry

How can we control our lives
We whined over the phone between Boston and West Virginia.
Then you read me your poem which you said was optimistic
And had a constructive point to make
About the tomato seed in the peat pot
Who made it on the first try
Without homework or formal education
And produced fruit
From each slender wrist.

FRUIT
I saw hanging from every ledge along Mass Ave
Blossoms nudging parking meters
Tiny green heads tapping on doors
Then
Big bomber tomatoes splitting store windows
Tomato traffic
Look out below
Vines make their way through stony Connecticut
Leaping the Hudson, choking refineries
Sidling over the turnpikes
Bending sharp southward into the Appalachians.

Now the red and green tide rumbles up my valley
Juicing through birches
Leaving skin on the oaks, pulp on the fence
Fat red and sliceable green
Phloem and xylem all over the porch in vascular bundles
Inside out and out of control.
They won't get me I said slamming the door

Puffing and sucking up through the floor boards
Listen, I might drown
I mean REALLY
In my house!
I thought about Life Saving, Junior and Senior
Surprised by Beefsteaks and Burpee Big Boys
Overwhelmed by tomatoes
Glub, blub...

Cut.
I said, cut.
I said CUT!

—Devon McNamara
Originally appeared in
THE HIRAM POETRY REVIEW

ASLEEP

I went to sleep on the couch
and woke up in the car
I went to sleep on a rainbow
and woke up in money
I went to sleep gross and
woke up grotesque
I went to sleep in fire
and woke up on Cloud 9.
I went to sleep on the beach
and woke up in the ocean
I went to sleep in jail and
woke up free
I went to sleep on an iron
and woke up depressed.

—Eric Reese

THE MOUTH

Braces flying
Teeth running
Tongues jumping.

—Jim Ross

FAMOUS DEAD PEOPLE

a poem letter

To Whom it May Concern:

I was wondering what it would be
like to be famous and even more, dead.
To be famous, is it like being
popular, or is it more like being
wanted, or could it be like feeling
needed?
To be famous and dead, do you
still feel famous, do you still feel
known, or do you feel forgotten, un-
needed, deserted, or as if you never
had been famous? Could it be that you
feel like an old tire rotting
in a field?

P.S.
Write Soon!

—John Sherman

CHATTAHOOCHEE

In the condemned apartment
where used kleenex drape the floor
A poor family talkes about
someday going to the river
talking about
walking to the river, where man
is free, free to live

Until one dies.

—Make Nass

HAND POEM

I thought I had a cap on my hand
all along it was a handicap on my back
I thought my hand
was made from man
but all along it was a handyman
I thought it was fractured by a man,
but he told me it was manufactured
He made my hand
and turned out a handmade hand
I thought my hand was handled
by both of my hands
but it is only handled
by my right hand
Left hands are strong
big and long
Right hands are rough
weak small and short
Since we don't have no more hand words
our phalanges are our fingers and
they go to our poems.

—Kim Penwell & Missy Baker

UPSIDEDOWNSIDESIDESIDEBOTTOMSIDEDOWN

The importance of voting in the water:
you can sing as you shoot eyes in the
circle, any white person can plant
fireseeds in his mouth, the camels can
graze in the oil slicks, the clerics can
throw crosses at the sideshow, and the
President can get his lungs blown away
by some guy who loves Jodi Foster.

—David Hellard

WRITING RIGHT

A person can never
right
it all down
to the extent of the meaning
how can we say the things that we think?
maybe it's hard for me, not you
except
to
ignore the fact
can be true

—Ann Obinger

THE GAME WAS TIED IN THE LAST INNING

The ball game was on fire in the last
inning.
The pitcher went around in a circle to
show the fans that he still had some
humor. He opened his mouth and yawned.
He kicked up some grass seed and then
got set and put his eye right on the
catcher's mitt. Then he had to use the
restroom and he crossed his legs and
said this is one time I don't need water
and soon as he said that a big bunch of
dusty air blew into his mouth.

—David Murphy

SOMETHING I KNOW WITH NO NAME

An empty school
A deserted city
A sunny night
A dark day
A modern painting
The feeling of wool
The feeling of a cold morning
Looking at a fire
Jumping in the air
Hitting the baseball solid
The feeling of falling

—Danny Diers

Aullwood Poems

THE CIRCLE OF ROCKS

We sat
and watched the birds
and life.
We listened
for animals that were all
around. So many interesting
things in life
unowned.

—Sabrina Allbecker

ONE DAY

As the water flows
under the bridge
people pass by quickly
and are all worried about time
and it becoming dark
they are trying to see the beauty of life
and the birds flying by
at the pond people rushing around
slipping and sliding
the flowers are blowing away
and sticky pollen
flies softly to the ground

—Patty Loos

COUNTRY EYES

Holding hands watching the ocean.
Horses galloping across the country.
Sounds of music at a foreign wedding.
A dog yelping, because he's hurt.
Sitting in a smoke-filled bar
Down in Kentucky or Tennessee.
When I'm down in the country it's like a dream.
It was a bitter harvest when our cows died.
My sister married a foreign agent.
I saw them holding hands watching the ocean.
I'm sitting thinking of this
in a smoke filled bar.

—Lori Green

POISON CONTROL

Whenever I say
Hi
You always
Make me
Eat just
Wooden Objects
Maybe
A good
Nutritious meal would please me.

—Mike Nalley

HORSE

The horse runs weightless
  Through the reign,
The horse runs courageously
  in grief without breath,
The horse is atomic with a
  seizure through the tropic
The horse is tumbling over
  the hills of green
The horse is running, running,
His vein is coming out
It's out! He's weightless.

—Stacy Rodgers

Southwestern High School
Gallia County

ODE TO CLASS

I went to class one fine morning
The teacher there started growling
Like a bear because of
  people throwing spit wads
  to the front of the room
  and making them stick
  one the wall
  like tar on a feather.
Then I went to fourth period
  to write this poem
  and relieve some
  stress
At least all classes are
  almost finished.
Ode to class.

—John Howe

LONELY BOY IN THE WOOD

Every night I will walk
in
the woody wet
dark woods
unless I find
a little lonely
girl to walk with me
and I will take her home
because I am nice
and honest boy in the woody woods.

—Chad Lewis

THE THREE OF LIFE

I'm trying to climb up the big bean tree
It's my very, very first time.
It's everybody else's too.
I'm already half way up.
I look back then ahead
Some are lingering and relaxing
They're afraid to go higher
Some are way ahead
Others have fallen
"Don't go on the branches," they always say
But some do. They hang by the leaves
And do flip flops
They creep back or fall.

I just sort of ease along
I wibble, I wobble, I slip and I slide
I laughed I giggle, I love and I cry
Just like one always does when trying
Something new
Sometimes I get attached to a spot
And think I want to stay
But the people behind are pushing
Making me go on
Like I sometimes find myself doing
To others
Some get caught and hand in the air
Others reach the top
  Everybody is trying for the top
But why?
  One up there is only one thing to do
JUMP!
That's beginner's luck.

—Deborah McCartney

FIRST TIME

My first time ever
playing putt-putt golf
  matter of fact it was the first time
    my dad ever bragged on me
The first time in love
  my mother bragged on me

HOW I FELT STAYING AT THE HOSPITAL

I was feeling so bad having to go see my father at the hospital. It hurt to see him in the way he was in. All I could see at first was a lot of things hook up to him. It was hard for me to talk to him. And when I was setting outside to see him again it was so lonely out there to set. I was just like I was about a hundred or more miles away. And now we are all home again. But I still feel a hundred miles away. It is just like being shut out of the family and my friends. It feels like I am gone so far away that no one can get a hold of me.

—Ann Thacker

In my opinion
to be truly happy
the first thing you must do is
give up love and putt-putt golf.
    Now on my oblivious way through life
     I'm so damn happy
      I could twist somebody's head off.

—Rick Silvers

INSIDE AND OUTSIDE

In the classroom
my skin is beginning to turn black
outside the light is hitting my hair
as the sun is hitting my back

the trees are begging to sway
as the leaves turn green
the sky is moving fast
as the sun falls down

my skin is turning red and white
and there's gold hair on my arm
and the silver leaves shine
this is the life
I spit over my left shoulder
Luck.

—Allen Green

NOT A THING

Not a writer
Not a singer
Not a thing
Just a student

Not a singer
Just a writer
Just a student
Click click

Just a writer
Just a singer
Click click

Dropped pen
Just a singer
Dropped pen
Not a writer
Not a thing.

—Jerry S.

FISHING

at our pond hooked a bass
Someone's singing
on the road
then hooked a boot

Someone's singing
Someone walking
then hooked a boot
I can't get it

Someone walking
it is beautiful
then hooked a boot
I fell in

it is beautiful
I fell in
fishing at our pond hooked a bass
on the road.

—Dean Cline

SUN SPOTS

sun burned
shoulders
I can't hear
beach
girls

I can't hear
I can't control myself
girls
Is it here?

I can't control myself
shout up
it's here
girls

shout up
girls
sun burned shoulder
beach

—Leo McCombs

THE ACCIDENT

I need an ink pen
I just yelled at someone
Can in the flowerpot
Sun on the horizon

I just yelled at someone
She just got an idea
Sun on the horizon
The rainbow in the water

She just got an idea
The name on the board
The rainbow in the water
An egg in his hand

The name on the board
An egg in his hand
I need an ink pen
Cat in the flowerpot.

—Maggie Pinkerman

THE END

The earth is shaking
do you like me?
it's the end
yellow flowers grow in spring

do you like me?
the rain comes down
yellow flowers grow in spring
let's sing

the rain comes down
the field is dry
let's sing
the evergreen's bow

the field is dry
the evergreens bow
the earth is shaking
it's the end.

—Gina Silvers

HAIR OF THE DOG

Hair of the dog
running through the field
the sun is shining
falling limbs from the trees

running through the field
water falling
falling limbs from the trees
the sound of rain

water falling
getting muddy
the sound of rain
the dog is dead

getting muddy
the dog is dead
hair of the dog
the sun is shining

—Allen Green

HOT ROD IDIOT

Cut out on the blacktop
Out to the dragstrip
Up and down it
Grab gears and go
Always in the lead
Rip up the pavement into pieces
Climb up the speedometer
Accelerator on up
Roaring engine under the hood
Stop you moron I'd like to live longer.

—Jerome Potter

THE BRINK OF DISCOVERY

While dining at a downtown sewage plant
  I met a French speaking briefcase
  After a short talk I asked for a menu
  They handed me a periodic table
  I ordered a medium rare magnesium sulfide steak
  with a die order of French fried florine
  and a huge super silicone sulfide salad
For desert we each had an order of radioactive cobalt
  It was a glowing experience!
We both spent the rest of the evening
  running to the bathroom
We saw the guest speaker
  walking toward a speeding sign
at the magnificent speed of 100 mph.

—Chris & Jeff

CHILD ABUSE

Call Mr. Harrison
Ring the neck of the cat
The house will tell all

The child cries
The screaming starts
The house will tell all

A siren sounds
The carpet is stained
A mother cries
The house will tell all.

—Teresa Arrowood

ARROWHEAD FEVER

I walk into the battle ground
where my objective
a fluted arrowhead
lies
upon a muddy pedestal
which has been waiting for the finder.
I pick it up
half of it still in the mud
As I pull
I hope for it to be all there
But no it is broken
Lost to another time
  which I will never see
only to hope to find the other piece
Is the real treasure
And it draws the finder on
Because you know it is either there or not
That is the bait
From which you get the Fever.

—Michael Bailey

SMILE TEST

Name____________________

1. Smiles are to be used:
    a. when you don't want to smile
    b. when you really want to smile
    c. when you ask for a favor
    d. none of the above
    e. all of the above

2. The best type of smile is a
    a. funny laugh
    b. dirty laugh
    c. stupid laugh
    d. none of the above

3. Diane was a little girl
She was at the circus.
A clown came up to her.
She laughed read hard.
What kind of laugh is this?
    a. dirty smile
    b. happy smile
    c. crystal clear smile
    d. none of the above
    e. all of the above

Score____________________

—Thomas Savage

LISTEN TO THE SILENCE

Who can I turn to?
Everything is so dark
How long must I go on?
Is there anyone listening

Everything is so dark
Somewhere in the night
Is there anyone listening
If there's something I can't have

Somewhere in the night
I only want it more
If there's something I can't have
It's the truth
I only want it more
It's the truth
Who can I turn to?
How long must I go on?

—Brenda

MY FIRST KISS

My first kiss was utterly
full of depravity
If felt so morose
just being kissed by him was
nefarious
He had a bellicose attitude
and was awfully
pugnacious
His kiss was terribly pernicious, but
It was venal.

—Shelly

PO-UH TREE

It's hard to do when you're told to write
It don't come and go like the switch on a light
You sit there and try real hard to think
But all you can do is sit there and blink.
You sit there and wonder "am I the only one?"
"Who hasn't got this stupid poem done?"
But you look through the room, row to row.
And find people writing, ever so slow.
A scribbled line here, a small word there.
Some just scribble without a care.
Then after a while she takes them all up
And attempts to make sense of "a crack in a cup."
Written by someone who's only half here
Who never heard of a guy called Shakespeare.
She'll see a deep meaning hidden inside
And show everyone with nothing to hide
She's a real nice lady who writes po-uh tree
I guess it's alright, it just ain't for me.

—Robert Price

CHILD KILLING IN ATLANTA

A
woman
cries, her
tears they flow
Her child is dead
No flowers grow. And
Is it really all in vein
that she should suffer so
much pain? The day before
there was no son, but still
her tears go on and on and
children die like
swatted flies and
somewhere else
a woman
cries.

—Tony Bently
Grade 9

Hannan Trace High School

THE FILM ON THE GLASS

I used to think a hero
was someone who could
light up my eyes on Saturday
morning

Now I think a hero is
someone who can see their
best friend trip out on
angle dust and feel no remorse

I used to think emotions
were something you let
burst out on impulse

No I think for some reason
emotions are something
that are locked in a huge
steel vault in the dark
deep pit

I used to think marriage
was a lifetime arrangement
with total devotion

Now I think marriage
is nothing more than
legally living together
for the sake of pride

I used to be a very small tree
with lots of leaves and very few branches
but now I am large
and my branches and trunk are infested
with insects
I used to be a cool glass of water
crystal clear
and very tall
but now I've evaporated
and all that's left is the film
on the glass.

—Tony Bently
Grade 9

NICHOLAS F. MUSKA b. 1942
534 Nesslewood Elem and Sec
Toledo, OH 43610
(419) 246-1249

Nick Muska holds degrees in literature and English from Antioch College and the University of California, Santa Barbara. He has participated in poetry festivals and workshops in France, England, and the Netherlands, as well as here in the U.S.A. In 1979, as Head Artist / Coordinator of the Art Commission of Greater Toledo's Inmate Arts Program, he teaches creative writing workshops in the county jail and prison farm. His first collection of poems, *Elm,* grew our of his experience as an industrial warehouseman in Toledo. During the past 15 years his work has appeared in such periodicals as the *Chicago Review,* the *Wabash Review, Rockbottom,* and the *Ocooch Mountain News.* In 1980, he edited and published *From Inside Out,* a collection of inmate writing. He is the recipient of two individual artist fellowships in creative writing from the OAC.

KEY WEST HILL

O when I die
let me die
with my white pants on
a good suntan
and cognac in my veins.
My family strolling by my side
all old lovers married to good men
or wrapped in the arms of loving women.
Let me take my last walk
on this earth
in the face of such beauty
and not be numb to it
But all, just once
to kiss it, for once for the last time
of my final time.

—Nick Muska
from 28 Sunsets and 4
All-Nite Taxi Rides,
a work in progress

The Blue Diamond
King. King of Spades. Ruling.
Blue. Blue is his diamond.
Diamond. His treasure.
Today it is here.
Tomorrow it shall be gone.
King Edward. King of Spades.
King of his blue treasure. The diamond.

—Kim Hornick
Grade 8

ELASTIC LOVER

Today it is always the lover
So elastic like a rubber band
People change like the devil
Yesterday, the lover was a devil
Today the devil is the lover
Elastic—like a rubberband.

—Jodie Errett
Grade 8

I WISH

I wish I lived in a green house
out in the country where I could listen
to the birds singing.
I wish I had an orange cat that
lived with me on Edith Avenue and could
sit and listen to the radio with me.
I wish I had a violet violet that held
Rod Daily in the middle of it, while listening
to the radio.
I wish I had a father that dresses in
his favorite color—red, and listened to Bach
with me.
I wish I had my best friend to sit and
listen to me play Beethoven on the brown
baby grande piano like he used to.
I wish I had my father back in his old
work blue jeans listening to me read something
I wrote myself.

—Jackey Sith
Grade 8

I WISH I KNEW HIM

I wish I knew him
His past and present fears
I wish I knew the answers to his problems
The reasons for his anger
The causes of his bruises
The makings of his pain
I wish I knew how to help him,
Help himself.

I wish I knew him
His past and present feelings
I wish I knew his family and closest friends
His hopes and his dreams
His successes and his failures
His love and his hate

I wish I knew how to help him,
Help himself.

—Steve Brunner
Grade 9

Wathching Larwen Swelk is like hearing Ethel Merman singing in the nude.

—Kevin Lindsey
Grade 8

RAIN

Your tears have been
falling
For quite some time now.
Yet people just go on
with their lives.
Trying to stay out of
your way.

—Teresa Tussing
Grade 9

PREPS

A preppie here,
A preppie there,
Do they wear
Izod underwear?

They're clean and wholeseome and
Brush with crest,
and there's *always*
an alligator on
their chest.

The ultimate preppie
wears pink and green
In polysester
they're *never* seen.

They'd never waste
Time at the local pub,
But are always seen
At the "tennis club".

With names like
Bunny, Muffy and Skip,
It's just enough to
Make you flip.

And this fuss well end
Sooner or later and it's
All because of an
    Alligator

—Colleen Sullivan
Grade 9

WINTER LOOK

A green house
White snow layer covers roots
Big white flakes
Fall and cover trees
While snow on street
slushes.

—Mike Strunk
Grade 8

I'M JUST ME

I'm just me when I talk for hours
And say nothing or
Walk for miles and take no steps
or get no place.
I'm just me when I'm sad or mad
and shed no tears. Oh I can't help
it I'm just me.
Yeah I'm just me when something is not
funny, yet, I roll
on the floor with the laughter.

I'm just me when my friends are in trouble
And I stick my "nose" in it though I
don't understand
Yeah I'm just me when I'm not hungry
Yet munch all night or say I'm
Not tired yet sleep for hours
I can't help it I'm just me.
Or when I fight and throw no
punches
Hum to a song I don't even know
Dance around and make no movements
I can't help it "I'm just me".

—Beth Nolan
Grade 9

CAROLYN

Carolyn
looks
through
glass bay windows
    that
magnify things,
    that
magnify words
on a page,
    that
magnify people
much larger than
    they
really are
    the
bay windows
supposedly
    help
her see
    she
needs to
    look
through
portholes.

—Angela Shores
Grade 9

ANITA

Anita
knows
partly what
it means
to be a different
hue
to have a
knife stab
her
pride

but

her strong autumn
face is
always
pointed up.
She often watches the
winter people fall.

—Angela Shores
Grade 9

ICECYCLES

A shiny
hanging
dagger,
Step,
if you dare!

—Lori Fleck
Grade 8

SPANISH TRANSLATION

Super submarine sandwich
  Ham, bacon, cheese, lettuce
  is this a sandwich or a deli
  Hold the onions, please
Oh, hot peppers, carrots, tacos
Salmon eyes, a page of Algebra
a piece of a vending machine, a banjo string;
Smell that aroma.

Gracious Amigo, with all respect,
Gracious, Gracious.

—Greg Price
Grade 8

MICRODOT BAT

Yesterday the microdot bat bit the
green vein of a cactus
Drawing the juice from the drying desert
beneath the blazing sun of Arizona
during the calm cool nite the vein bat
disappeared. Today, june,
in a microdot second.

—Niki Trytko
Grade 8

LIFE

Run from death
Luck be with you
Faster and faster life rushes on
Work is a storm of the mind
Children are playing
Don't even look, hurry by
Wait
Death has beaten you
You've lost the race and wasted
Your life.

—Samantha Bloodhard
Grade 9

MY SISTER

Her voice clangs out,
loud and clear like a cracked
school bell.
No wind needed.
It just erupts from within.
Debbie bellows louder than life
earth shakes,
windows rattle,
birds self-destruct.
And that's only her whisper,
Lord help us!!

—Tricia Gallagher
Grade 9

HOSE HEAD

Hose head
a man so brave
Hose head
bites 20c stamps in two
Hose head
limps along with feet in
pockets
Hose head
lives for the sake of socks
Hose head
you're such a "hose head"!

—Lori Fleck
Grade 8

My knees pop like the hiss
of a fire.
My eyes are alive with a
burning fury.
My feet are like a scorched
old log.
My face is charred coal
black
Burning away is my look
itself
What is this world
coming to?

—Lori Fleck
Grade 8

MY FINGERS SPURT FIRE LIKE A VOLCANO

My book on fire melts in my hand
I leave my trail of wax books
along the way
I feel my mind boiling like a
kettle of water
I see myself melting away.

—Lisa Baldwin
Grade 8

BURNT TOAST

A feeling of standing at a funeral
Listening to the preacher.
Hearing the squeal of a dog
As a truck runs over his foot,
The feeling of watching him
Hold his leg and hobble home.

A feeling of your boyfriend calling
And saying "I don't feel we
should see each other anymore."
The feeling that swept you,
When you found your older sister
Had her first baby and it was stillborn.
The feeling of your parents telling you
They don't feel they could live
Together much longer.
They feel you will have to choose
Which parent.

The feeling of taking your toast
out of the toaster and finding
out it's burnt.

—Lori Fry
Grade 9

TODAY—THE TRANSPARENT PRESENT

Yesterday, death was the opaque future,
Today, death is the transparent present.
The guilotine stands tall on the wooded platform,
Waiting to behead the insane murderer.

The saxophone's slow music is mournful,
While the killer steps up to the treacherous guillotine
As he puts his head upon the harsh blade's edge,
You can see the dark secrets hidden in his
mysterious green eye.

No longer does sound seep from the saxophone,
The world is silent and mourning.
Yesterday, death was the opaque future,
Today, death is the transparent present.

—Kristi Struble
Grade 8

REDDING OF A REDNECK

The red of my blood
The red of my heart
My red love
On that red neck.
Take your red luscious apple
And your red love fruits.

I'll keep my red hot love
for the perfect one.
I wouldn't give you
A red cent of love.
or a kiss from red cherry lips.

—Gwen Sullivan
Grade 9

UNDERARM DEODORANT

Today the underarm deodorant
was sitting on a blue shelf
in a blue bottle. It was
waiting to be used and then
got dropped on the floor.

Yesterday it was still sitting
in a Florida supermarket waiting
to be picked up by a woman.

Then it got picked up and
dropped. It was put into a big
brown shopping bag waiting to
get home. Look where he
ended up today. On another shelf
waiting to be used.

—Missy Dunn
Grade 8

JEFF OLMA
219½ Locust Street
Perrysburg, OH 43551
(419) 352-1834
(419) 666-0580 x 393

Elem and Sec

Jeff is a Buffalo, NY native with a passion for hockey and writing. He has an MFA from Bowling Green State University and is currently an assistant professor of communications and humanities at Owens Technical College, Toledo. He has taught language arts and reading at all levels and has worked in the Toledo area Young Authors Program as well as the OAC's AIE program. His work has appeared in many periodicals, including MEASURE, FIREWEED, THE GREENHORSE REVIEW FOR POETRY, SALTHOUSE, and ITINERARY II.

after reading

after reading a letter
from an old friend
i am thinking
that time is a queer bird.

memory takes us back
to good old days,
alarm clocks and schedules
take us by the hand
through the tasks of our ways,
and wishes
propel us toward some star
of moments
which we can only dream about.

and yet
all of these times
exist together
like elevator riders
shoulder to shoulder,
space filled, then
emptied out
onto various 4th floors
of the Now and Then
Department store.

—Jeff Olma

I thought I'd make it good this time
I thought my time had come
I thought that this time
Would really be the one.
But just like I had returned
To all the years before
This summer—my vacation
Turned into a total bore.

—Kay Fisher

THE FIRST DAY

I woke up today
Kind of early I suppose
But there was a reason
I wipe my eyes and look over to my right
A pair of new designer jeans
And my favorite shirt all laid out
Nice and neat
Oh gee—how could I forget this day
Well—I jump out of bed
And go wash my face
Look at those bags under my eyes
And the two zits—one on my nose, the other on my check
Oh well—I've got my trusty make-up
Not much improved on my methods
It goes on somehow
I give up after awhile
Even though I'm not satisfied with the way I look
Over to the breakfast table now
Which is the living room floor of course.
With people I don't even know
Telling me good morning on the tv set
Grape Nuts sound good to me
So I grab a bowl and crunch and crunch

Now don't forget to make your bed
And turn on the stereo
Cause I'm still not awake
On go my clothes
Oh gee—kind of tight
And I said I'd be skinny by today
HA—Another stupid attempt to lose weight
Ugh! My hair I've got to brush through it
At least 10 more times—at least!
I'm walking out the door now
Grouch to my mom
I couldn't fall asleep the night before
And now I look like a mess
Yuck!
10 months later (it seems)
I reach my friend's house
A laugh here and there and we're there
Check out all the fancy duds
Half of them don't know what's going on
Walk inside—ding a ling
Sitting at a desk
Pencil in hand writing
Already! Gee—Give me a break!
There's Jeff. He's waving and winking
Oh God—not another year of this?
There's Scott, by Jeff! WOW!!
Same old Scott.
I think he actually smiled at me
Great!
Lunch—I skipped of course
Who needs nutrition at school?
Who even gets it at this cafeteria?
HI everyone!!
Back here again for another 9 months
Just like being pregnant—
Gotta carry it through—
All the pain, joy, fun times, suffering, etc.
then LET IT OUT!!!!!!

—Kay Fisher

GAMES

I was serving into the deuce court,
we were even
back and forth
until you took a chance
and tried to pass me,
but it only left you
"add out"

I guess having the advantage
scared me
I couldn't face being ahead
double fault
back to deuce,

You went on to win that—
teasing me
with drop shots and lobs
and then we were back to love

Who says
Love isn't a game?

—Rebecca Fariss

SECRET DREAMS NOBODY KNOWS

Secret dreams nobody knows
Taken by black death
to the hell below me.
No one understands why
I discontinue contact,
But you see...nobody knows me.

Sometimes I fly in purple skies.
Sometimes I cling to orange trees.
As you can tell,
my mind is not in reality.

My world is sometimes cold.
Secret dreams nobody knows
My soul given to insane spirits,
Shivering—tied raw to steel poles.

Spirits digging to get my blood.
Secret dreams nobody knows...
staked down to the ground covered in mud,
people don't understand why
I always think of death,
But you see—in this cold, cold world
you never know what you'll get.

Secret dreams nobody knows
Taken by black death
to the hell below me.

—Fawn Butte

I'M JUST AN OLD PAIR OF COWBOY BOOTS

I have taken your abuse,
Stood in the rain with you
Endless hours waiting for concerts.
Walked with you through mud.
Gone with you to many a good time
We have shared more than could be remembered.
Just you and me.
Afterall,
What are cowboy boots for?

—Angie Middleton

Ringing.
I turn my head and open my eyes
while reaching for a button
that controls my day.

—Joe Arras

SCHOOL

The people arrive in swarms
Like ants on a piece of bread.
These swarms then move slowly around
From room to room to room,
Each time stopping, just long enough
To make them want to start again.
They receive assignments to be done at home
That must be complete at any price.
What kind of place is this that makes so many people
want to attend to be punished?

—Shannon Clark

GARY PACERNICK
Dept. of English
Wright State University
Dayton, OH 45431

(513) 873-2443 (W)
(513) 236-2341 (H)

Elem and Sec

Gary Pacernick has published poems in such magazines as THE AMERICAN POETRY REVIEW, NORTH AMERICAN REVIEW, POETRY NOW, and THE CHARITON REVIEW. His work has been anthologized in *Travelling America with Today's Poets, Poems Within the Ark: Modern Jewish Poets, 73 Ohio Poets,* etc. His verse play *I Want to Write a Jewish Poem* has been produced on stage and on public television. He is a former member of the OAC's literature advisory panel, the editor of IMAGES, a poetry tabloid, and teaches English at Wright State University.

THE AIR FORCE MUSEUM

Three hundred Baptist Sunday school children
Are hanging from the wings of the giant B-36.
A line of families waits to enter
"The world's most decorated bomber:
1,500,000 tons of bombs on target."
It's a mausoleum of bombshells,
Meters, dials, belts, tin seats.
A man stops to aim a turret gun.
Back outside, a tiny observation plane
Hovers in mid-air from the ceiling.
"The Strawberry Bitch" is tattooed to the ribs of a fighter bomber.
There are pictures of the Glenn Miller Band
And momentoes of World War II prisoners of war:
A cardboard pendulum clock, a soldier's painting of the blue Venus,
Notes pencilled on the back of cigarette wrappers, a poem.
The movie of the day shows an Eighth Air Force bomber crew
Dodging black flak over Germany for the twenty fifth time,
Dropping bombs on the enemy's factories and bridges.
This is the dark Disneyland of war waiting to be reborn.

—Gary Pacernick

STORY

Deep valley
flowered & fired
travel along the path
twisting
turning
see the stallion
raise on two feet
then one
then away!
Silent no more is there life as you walk?
follow a butterfly
see it dance
painting shadows onto he ground
watch it dance
then see it flutters slowly away to the sun
walk slowly now
see and hear nothing but your footsteps
nothing
silent
walk over the valley hill to see...
a city.
How beautiful, how open are the gates.
Then clash!
They close.
You walk away and see nothing but pale hills.
You walk slowly away,
very slowly.

—Melissa Johnson

In an enchanted land
where the flowers are as big as trees
all around me like a jungle
then I come upon a lake
crystal clear the sparkling water
ripples over my feet
I bend down and pick up
a shell and open it. Inside
there is a perfect pearl.
It is the size of a golf ball.
I hold it up to the sun
and it reflects light.
It drops into the lake
slowly sinking to the bottom
gone from me forever.

—Chris Kessler

I went down to the sea one day,
and I saw a cloud over the water.
It was shaped like a lamb,
it was quiet,
it was slowly moving across
the golden sky,
for it was beginning to get dark
I sat there in the dark
sunrise the next day
and the lamb was gone,
nowhere to be seen,
it slowly...quietly...gently...
floated away...

—Kim Campbell

THE SEA

The air is dark and cold.
The sea is black as oil.
Then a thousand seagulls fly up straight
and the sun rises in the sky
like a thousand blooming flowers
that break the dark and cold.
The sea turns gold.
The air is warm.

—Andy Fenic
8th grade

THE SEA

I was looking over the railing of our ship;
It was the dead of night.
The sea was calm at times but at times
it rose up into a great flurry and
thrashed at the side of the ship.
I was not alone but with the sea.
Then the moon showered it's rays
onto the glistening water.
The wind blew my hair furiously,
And once again the sea tried to
destroy our ship and then quieted down.
Now the wind was slow and soft, and
the sea was quiet and the moon
shone on my face.
I was not alone but with the sea.
I felt like a seagull ready for flight.

—Amy Wirtanen

KILLER WHALES

The mates came running to the deck
To see a school of killer whales
Suddenly they thought they had better
  save the diver's neck
The school of fish came on so fast
They hadn't a minute to think.
Some of the mates were blasting them
But most of them were trying to
  pull in the diver.
It ends in a tragic way.
The line to the diver snaps
And he is lost in the school of whales.

—Heather Backer

THE JIMGILLMEWGIR

The jimgillmewgir is a strange beast,
For it faces north and south and west and east.
The reason for this is rather plain,
It has four heads, I won't say it again.
Its transportation isn't very quick,
It hops around on a pogo stick.
It has a head of a Chesire cat, a
  giraffe, a Jimmy Carter, and a fish
And for predators it's not an appetizing dish.
The reason why the predators don't
  gobble this beastie up,
Is because they're aren't any.
I made it up!

—Howard Forbes

HERBERT SCOTT
Department of English
Western Michigan University
Kalamazoo, MI 49008
(616) 383-1717

Elem and Sec

Herb has a BA from Fresno State College and an MFA from the University of Iowa. He has taught in college and also worked as a retail grocer. He is the author of two poetry collections, *Disguises* and *Groceries,* both from the University of Pittsburgh Press. His work has been widely anthologized as well as published in numerous periodicels including HARPER's POETRY, PLOUGHSHARES, and NORTH AMERICAN REVIEW.

SCHOOLING

Late afternoon the children
come in from school.
All day they have eaten
the sorrow of small rooms
the tragedy of textbooks
until their stomachs spin
like the skies over battlefields.

In the sweet aisles
their empty hands
pulse like hearts
their bodies open like gates
to fill with the flood of goods.
At suppertime they founder
in the laps of their fathers.

—Herb Scott

Stranahan Elementary School

Fourth Grade

Self-Portraits

WHAT I AM!

I'm a piece of pizza with *no* mushrooms
and extra pepperoni and sausage.
People say I am shy, but I'd really like to fly.
I like to swim in a gym with a hot tub and four
guys all *MINE*.
I'm a little country and a lot of rock and roll.
People say I'm a genius, but I say
at least I'm good looking.

—Tabitha Carter

ME, MYSELF, AND I

I woke up early this morning, dressed in blue.
I looked up in the sky and I saw a bluebird flying by.
Then in front of my eyes it began to rain
on the tops of the trees.
It's the ending of summer and the
beginning of fall.

—Chris Nevers

I am a season of fall when the leaves fall
  and turn colors like red, yellow, green.
I like to eat the water that people sprinkle on me.
I like when the wind blows.
I go every where the wind goes.

—Carolyn Levitan

THE HOT SUMMER DAY

I am a hot summer day waiting for winter to end.
I am people wating to get a nice red tan.
I am trees wating to get leaves back.
I am roses wating and wating and wating for winter
  to end.
I am an orange wating to be eaten.
I am a termite wating to get fresh wood.
I am a bird wating to get a worm.
I am a car wating to be driven again.

—Dean Lewis

MW

I am a ham, extra cheese omelet.
I am a 20 horse power gocart.
I am a BMX bike driver.
I am a hotdog, plain.
I am a TV set with all channels.
I am a Z28 with a turbo engine.

—Kevin Berg

FALCON

I fly with the wind with my wings
  spread wide.
I swoop down and get field mouse
  running through the pasture.
I live in a big red wood tree in
  Canada.
I have three new baby falcons.
I have dark red and brown feathers.
I can see 250 feet above and far away.
Man is my worst enemy.
I glide through the air with the winds
  blowing my feathers.

—David Wetmore

ALL ABOUT FISH

It's wonderful to be a fish.
I like to swim a lot.
I like to eat fish food because I am a fish.
My secret hiding place is in the shell because
  I don't like to be disturbed.
The color of me is gold.

—Sue Rinehart

NOSE

The nose is like a weapon
  It can smell.
The nose can be as red as an apple
  Or blood from a cut.
It can be as steep as the mountains
  In Vail that you ski down.
The nose can be as flat as a
  waxed floor.
It can be as fat as a mountain or
  an island.

—Jason Albring

FINGERS

Fingers are like little fat sticks.
They bend in three places.
They have hard nails like plastic.
They can count.
If a finger could talk, it would
  probably say, "Give me a break."
Finge s cen hotd things.
It would be hard to do things without
  them.
They hold the thumb;
  They bend like an elbow.
They don't have a sound;
  They feel bony.
It doesn't have a taste;
  It doesn't have a small.
I'm glad to have fingers.

—Jenny Baumhower

NOSES

Noses are stuffed
Noses are clean.
Noses bring air in
  like a vacuum machine.
Noses are red;
  Noses are peach.
Noses don't have any feet
Noses are round
Noses are slanted.
Noses may look
  Like a leaf on a plant.

—Jim Cassidy

THE TONGUE

Nobody likes the tongue
It comes out of the mouth
  Like a cobra out of its hole.
Bright red,
  As red as blood.
It can rub your teeth
  Like a pig rubbing
Its back against a fence.
It can play a flute
  And some other instruments.
For without a tongue,
  You could not talk.
You would eat like a slob
Without it.
So nobody likes a tongue
  Except for the person
Who's got it.

—Chris Colotto

THE MOUTH

Oh door of my head
  Why won't you stay shut.
Because of you
  I get in trouble
  And get yelled at.
You remind me of a door
  That cannot shut
And of a baby starling
  That is wating for its breakfast
  And will not hush.

—Rick Simon

FINGERS

Fingers are good to count
  From one to ten.
They can also be good
  To hold things.
Fingers are good for itches.
Without fingers
  Everybody would call you stubby.
You would have to rub agasint the wall
  To get rid of itches.
Your fingers can touch
  Every part of your body
If you didn't have fingers,
You couldn't say
  "This is finger lickin' good." .
Your fingers tell stories.
They're good for the deaf.

—Jason Klapfish

MY ANKLE

Oh ankle,
  You look so lonely.
You always have a bruise on you,
  Or your always being twisted.
Mr. Ankle,
  You always help my foot to walk.
When we march or when we play.
  Mr. Ankle,
You are so nice to my foot,
That you are the greatest.

—Beth Langenderfer

KNUCKLES

Oh knuckles,
  How we mistreat you by cracking you.
In a boxing match,
  We hit other people with you.
It would be hard to bend our fingers
  without you.

—Kevin Miller

FIST

Your fist is something to protect you.
  Your fist is something to throw a ball with.
  If you didn't have a fist
  What fun would boxing be?
A fist can tell you how big your heart is.
  A fist has 12 cousins—10 fingers
  and two wrists.
Fists are for puppets and playing with toys.
  If you didn't have a fist
How would you drive?
  If I had no fist you wouldn't be
reading this right now.

—John Burke

HEART

The heart is glazed
  Redhot with pumping every second.
Oh how you send friends everywhere.
  It makes my body run.
A red stream, a flowing river,
  You must never enter my liver,
Even though you are friends.
   Let's hope you never say out to
    lunch
For then I will fade away.
  Oh, please don't stop ticking today!

—Sean Gyuras

TEETH

The teeth are the bars of the jail,
  The tongue is in.
Without you, teeth
There would be no jail.
And who would fight the food
  That doesn't want to be swallowed?
Dentists hurt you by making holes
  And pulling you out.
They are sorry
  And teeth, who do you bite nice people?

—Jill Wolff

FRECKLE

The dot on my face like a zit.
  But it's not, it's brown.
Some people call it a freckle,
  Not me,
I call it ugly.
  It looks like someone took mud
    and threw it at me.

—D.J. St. Germain

SKIN

I am the skin.
  Without me you be a big pile of bones.
A am the one to keep your big bones from
  showing.
I come in different colors like a box of
  crayons.
And I come in different shapes like big,
   huge, tiny small, like an assorted
   box of toys.

—Brian Whalen

Images

THE TOP

You dream of the top the big leagues
  Now you're in the little league,
For baseball or basketball or even football.

In baseball you throw hard
  Though fast and not the last.
I can't make it over the plate
  I throw it too high or throw it too low.
Maybe even not at tall.
  I toss the basketball,
It arches in the air and bounces off.
  I realize I'll never make it there.
So I sigh in despair.

—David Yu

One day my fish was sick,
I saw him doing flips when I came home
from school.
It's a small gold fish with a black-lined fin.
I gave him two drops of medicine behind
the gills.
I thought he was all right until I came from
school again
And saw him floating on top.
I was sad as I threw him away.

—Chris Michaelis

SAD FACES

It was a disappointing rain.
Sad wet faces looked out of a black
Pontiac window
On the way up a tall mountain.

The streets of Killarney, Ireland lingered below.
We got to the top of the mountain
A medium, height, middle-aged man stepped
out of the car.
His two children followed.
We climbed the rocks
Examining the strange foliage
I looked out and absorbed the beautiful
green world.
I smiled and was happy again.

—Lisa Kelly

My cat, Pierre has a moustache.
  Like a handsome young man.
She has black dots on the tops of her ears
  Like earrings on a young lady.
She sits on the diningroom table
  To see the birds fluttering in the air.

—Jill Annarino

POLLUTION

If animals could talk
  What would they say?
I know, they would say, "Why has man polluted
    land?
  Why has man polluted the sea?
Pollution here, pollution there
  Look around it's everywhere.
If man would open up his eyes,
  He would see why everything dies.
Pollution, pollution, it's in the air
  And birds are dying, don't you care?
If you please, clean up this mess
  Or one day when you least suspect
We'll be gone forever more
  And I think it will be hard to shut
    that door."

—Gwen Walbolt

VIOLIN

I am a violin sitting on stage,
  Playing a very neat tune,
With a green silken dress and beautiful
  brown shoes.

I am music sitting on a stand,
  With a dot here and there,
I am a bow floating smoothly across
  the string,
And then I go home to my warm comfortable
  bed.

—Sheila Cook

The 4th desk in the first row is full of
  old math papers,
Scattered all around inside the desk.
  It's also got an old moldy sandwich
   in it.
It's like a garbage can,
  Full of jūnk or the cafeteria lunch.

—Brent Gilley

CHIN

A chin is a part of the body that doesn't
 really get noticed.
It just sits there like a drunk man on
 a park bench in New York.
Some chins are pointy.
 Some have a space in between.
Other people have two chins and some don't
really have one at all.
Some ladies put colored powder on their
 chin to make it look better.

—Wendy Clevenger

THE PENGUIN

I am a penguin,
 who wobbles like a football.
I'm cold and have an icicle hanging from
 my nose.
I sleep on icebergs with a frozen fish
 in my beak.
My iceberg floats out into the ocean,
 But when I wake I will do the back stroke.
Towards shore with a frozen fish in my beak.
 Then in a hollow beneath me,
I see a gray fin.
 It is the fin of a pin shark.
I hear him moving around.
 I am a little penguin floating to shore.

—Greg Knapinski

DAVID SHEVIN | b. 1951
2239 Flora St. | Elem and Sec
Cincinnati, OH 45219
(513) 421-6650

David is currently a staff worker for the American Federation of Television and Radio Artists. An alumnus of the New York State PITS program, he has been active with the OAC's Artists-in-Education program since 1975. Previously recipient of the Elliston Poetry Fellowship at the University of Cincinnati, he holds a BA from Lewis and Clark College and an MFA from Bowling Green State University. His poems, essays, and translations have appeared in many publications. Books include *What Happens, The Stop Book,* and *Camptown Spaces*.

POEM

boy leaning back
the red running shoes
tilt and touch in concentration
then slow and settle
like ripe jumping beans
come into shadow
at dusk

—David Shevin

Country Day School
Cincinnati

BUS POEM

A bus that is real simple to pick up.
A bus with purple and green tires.
A bus with an orange statue on the front bumper.
A bus with a chair on the roof.
A bus with 1 wheel.
A bus with a house on top.
A bus that is shaped like a bolt.
A bus with a painting in front.
A bus that is on a roller coaster.

—Eric Mays

LIKE THE LION

Like the lion some men are big and lazy. Like the lion some men's voices can be heard 5 miles away. Like some lions some men are mean, but yet like most lions some men are gentle. Actually like all lions some men care for things or people he knows. Like some lions some men have long hair. Like all lions some men have big muscles. Like lions some men have long, sharp nails.

—Marty Joe Dodson

ODE TO PIZZA

Ode to pizza, that delicious taste.
I savor it. I don't eat it in haste'
and never, ever will I waste
that delicious, nutritious pizza.

Some people say pepperoni
tastes like pepper only
and others say mozarella
tastes like ma's umbrella,
and people who love pimento
are a little dimento!

—Sapha Buder

HOW TO BE A DOLL

You always have to be still. Never breathe or blink your eyes unless you are electric. Take the pain and torture that is given to you. When little Buster comes along and tries out his new paint set on one of your eyes, or throws you around, don't you dare say a word.

And if you get too hungry, don't let a tear drop from your eyes. That is the way to be a doll.

—Kathy Cummings

HOW TO BE A TWO-HEADED OCTOPUS

Eat a baby octopus. Then
mix water, milk, raw egg, a
pinch of raw meat, and a little
syrup. Cut off one of your
hands and that will make
you sleep for exactly one hour.
When you wake up go to
the nearest ocean and swim in
the deepest part of all. When
you come out you will be
a two-headed octopus.

—Tracy Captain

JUST LEAVE ME ALONE

I wish everyone would leave
me alone. I don't need any
loving care.
Don't ask me if I want
a sweet,
Don't fix any of my
favorite things to eat.
Don't give me one bit of
advice.
But most of all just
don't be nice at all.
But when I have wallowed
well in sorrow
Be sure to be nice to me
tomorrow

—Jaylene Boland

SCIENTIST
(sung like "Oh My Darlin'")

The scientist, the scientist, who'll know
what he does. He's made some atomic
bombs and some other junk, too

They work with telescopes and some
cylinders, too. They were great and
kept forever, kept forever always

The computers and machines they work
like a dream. They answer all our
Questions, all our questions every time.

—Ethan

TEACHER'S SONG

The kids are nice to be around, but
there's one that no one can stand. He's
the little redhead throwing the paper
wads around. I'm trying to straighten him out,
but just think when I'm finished with this
I get to go home and make supper.

—Mary Remenosky

ANIMAL POEM

Bird as in tongue when a bird does
not have nowhere to go.
Cat as in nose when she's hungry and
does not have anything to eat when she smells
then she finds something.
Beak as in pig instead of getting messy of
eating he can pick it up with his
beak
Cave as in porcupine so you won't see it
dirty.
Bee as in dog like when a dog
barks it will not make noise.

—Dawn Rice

Indian Valley School
Enon

You drool on the steak
before you.
As your father says
grace you take your knife
and fork and cut off
a piece.
You slip it in your
mouth before your
father is done
Your mother hits you
You finish your steak
with a pain in your
face
You finish your potatoes
and give your asparagus
to your dog.
You leave the table
stuffed like a hog.

—Carol Robinson

ODE TO JOHN BELUSHI

A funny man who
made people laugh
We loved him for that.
He was famous but lonely.
He was mixed up and was messing
with the wrong stuff.
Now we all miss him very, very much
and we'll remember him...
forever.

—Beth Hoback

ODE TO MARILYN MONROE

A beautiful woman who
was loved by everyone.
A bright woman who couldn't
take the pressure of the image, "Star".
Her face will always be remembered,
and her smile never forgotten.
She couldn't handle all of
the people and things taking over her life.
I hope she's happy wherever
she is because she obviously
wasn't happy here.
It's a shame such a beautiful
and loving person took her life.
She had such a long life ahead of her,
but other ruineds ruined her...
forever!!

—Shelly Frish

MALCOLM X

He was born a poor black boy
—No joke intended there—
Poverty embedded in his soul
Born to drink, smoke, or swear.
But that's not what laid in store for him.
A preacher, a man in his soul
Until that cold, bleak afternoon
Where he was murdered
Buried in the knoll
He served his time in prison
For a crime he did commit
He belonged to a religion
The one that he saw hit.
He was a controversial figure.
Even he admitted that
He always did what he thought was right
If it meant putting up a fight.
He was never wrong in my eyes
I would've done the same
I probably would've too but he
Was dead long before I came.

—Kenny "Gonzo" Webb

ODE TO A BOOK

Thank you for bringing a new
adventure with each page.
For the times you made me
laugh and cry.
For when you took me to the battlefield,
the ends of the earth
and finally
to a peaceful mountain stream.

—Amy Ellis

BLACK

quiet death
an awful smell
a dark night

—Steve Arnold

MOUTH

An open hole in the ground
Surrounded by rocks and a rabbit
That peaks out once in a while.

—Chris Melton

OLD AGE

Old age is
the wrinkles on a raisin

—Kim Wunder

JIM VILLANI
P.O. Box 237
Youngstown, OH 44501
(216) 744-2258

b. 1948
Elem and Sec

Jim received his BA and MA in English from Youngstown State University. Since 1974 he has been editing and publishing PIG IRON magazine, a publicly supported literary journal. He currently teaches English composition at Youngstown State University. Recent publications include *Interstate, Abraxis, The Ohio Journal,* and *Artist's Pulp.*

THE DANCE

The soft, silvery dust of the moon's birth
Falls upon the gray bark of a dead tree,
Softly taps the arteries of its earth
Until empty arms begin to wave free,
Flailing fast against the blood sky, uproots
To sail wildly across the night-land;
In the distance a lone owl hoots,
Breaks the silence of night's dark hand.
All cautious movement now, in harmony
A flower sheepishly grins loves down sky;
And the creatures of night open their yellow
Lust eyes; then a soft pearl-yawn hastens by.
In love we are all children of the night.
In dreams the tears of desire master flight.

—Jim Villani

I am like a kite string.
I go where the wind will take me,
To the outer reaches of the atmosphere;
My mind flies away.
I have no restriction as to how far I go,
As long as someone is there to unwind me.
If no one is there to unwind me,
I become trapped, like a fish on a bowl,
able to go no farther.

—Fred Behnke

The branches of a tree in December
covered with snow
stand tall and erect
through the day and night
birds come here to perch
singing a song
The birds call to their mates
finding that they are close by
coming together
and choosing the branch
they wish to die on

—Karen Canfield

THE SOUND OF SNOW

The quiet of a winter's day
The stillness of a winter's night
The sharpness of a winter's breeze
All of these left untouched
But for the sound of falling
Snow that no one hears
It falls through the quiet of day
And the stillness of night.
It dances on the sharp winter breeze.
Nothing ever changes the sound
of snow that no one hears.

—Michele Black

Austintown-Fitch H.S.
Youngstown

IN THE NIGHT

A black mist
covers the light of day.
Shadows appear under street lamps
in the park.
Lovers lay on benches,
waiting for the moon,
Sparks hit the night,
suddenly everything
moces.

—John Thomas

ENRAGED ANGER

She yelled at me like thunder
Because I was on the phone
While she was waiting for her boyfriend to call.
Her windfull voice echoed throughout the house
She stormed from room to room,
Slamming the doors as she blew past.
Her footsteps were like the crash of rain.
Finally, her fury spent, she
Drifted away.

—Barb Cook

SCHOOL CAFETERIA

Students rush to the cafeteria
Like a herd of buffalo,
Only to be disappointed by the food.
The tables and floors are dirty.
The food is harsh.
The spaghetti is like eating earth-worms
Just surfaced from the cold wet ground,
With chunks of dirt still clinging to them.
The milk is like drinking lemon juice.
The pretzels are hard as drumsticks
And taste like dead branches.
The potato chips are like wet
Moldy leaves fallen from trees.
Students throw food,
Afraid to eat it.

—Pat Bigelow

MOUNTAINS

Sun sets behind it
The different colors
reflect off the snow caps
We want to paint a
mural on the Wall
Going down the
highway we see the mountains in
the distance,
Looking sad standing
alone.
Notice the different
colors and shades,
Feel our ears pop
when we drive up.
The cool crisp air
The wind whipping
around us
Look down on the
world.
Higher then everybody
The river looks like
a string of thread
Free, alone on the
mountains.
Thinking out your
problems,
No one knows
where we are.
With funny thoughts
going through our minds,
We feel like jumping
and gliding into the air.

—Dorie Parker
Grade 11

SCUBA DIVING

I enter the water
cool, calm, relaxed.
Swim deeper, the temperature drops.

The coral are mellow rainbows of color,
Fish flow gracefully like professional dancers.
I notice a shark, a wightless god levitating
But the massive warrior doesn't notice.

Time runs out, only five minutes
Of life sustaining air, relaxed,
But it takes fifteen minutes to decompress....

It's useless. I swim on
Getting light, my head spins,
Everything is so beautiful.

—Thomas Kirchbaum
Grade 11

You don't like my jeans
for your lips is curled and
your nose scrunched, like
a puppy confronted with an
unknown object.

—Becky Dougherty
Grade 12

HAIKU

Dragon kites flying
hirh in the sky. Cotton tails
lifting them higher.

—Becky Doughtery
Grade 12

DISCO

I saw you
on the dance floor.
Your limbs like
eind-blown branches.
Your legs like those
of a newborn colt.

—Becky Doughterty
Grade 12

BEAVERCREEK LOCAL SCHOOLS
2940 Dayton-Xenia Road
Xenia, OH 45385

BENJAMIN FRANKLIN ELEMENTARY SCHOOL
100 Broad Avenue
Findlay, OH 45840

BERNE UNION ELEMENTARY SCHOOL
506 N. Main Street
Sugar Grove, OH 43155

BIGELOW HILL ELEMENTARY SCHOOL
300 Hillcrest Avenue
Findaly, OH 45840

CENTRAL JR. HIGH SCHOOL
200 West Main Cross Street
Findlay, OH 45840

CHILLICOTHE CITY SCHOOLS
455 Yoctangee Parkway
Chillicothe, OH 45601

CLAY LOCAL SCHOOLS
Box 45, Route 6
Portsmouth, OH 45662

CLINTON ELEMENTARY SCHOOL
7927 Fulton Street
Clinton, OH 44216

DONNELL JR. HIGH SCHOOL
301 Baldwin Avenue
Findlay, OH 45840

FEDERAL HOCKING LOCAL SCHOOLS
Box D
Stewart, OH 45778

FINDLAY HIGH SCHOOL
1200 Broad Avenue
Findlay, OH 45840

FITCH HIGH SCHOOL
Falcon Drive
Youngstown, OH 44515

FOREST ELEMENTARY SCHOOL
28963 Tudor Drive
North Olmsted, OH 44070

FRENCH ART COLONY
Box 472
Gallipolis, OH 45631

GALLIA COUNTY LOCAL SCHOOL
220 Jackson Pike
Gallipolis, OH 45631

GALLIPOLIS CITY SCHOOLS
463 Second Avenue
Gallipolis 45631

GIBBS ELEMENTARY SCHOOL
1329 Gibbs Avenue
Canton, OH 44705

GLENWOOD JR. HIGH SCHOOL
1715 North Main Street
Findlay, OH 45840

HASTINGS JR. HIGH SCHOOL
1850 Hastings Lane
Upper Arlington, OH 43220

HOLMESVILLE ELEMENTARY SCHOOL
P.O. Box 8
Holmesville, OH 44633

HOWLAND LOCAL SCHOOLS
7200 South Street
Warren, OH 44484

INDIAN VALLEY SCHOOL
510 S. Enon-Xenia Pike
Enon, OH 45232

JONES JR. HIGH SCHOOL/UACAC
2100 Arlington Avenue
Columbus, OH 43221

LIBERTY UNION THURSTON ELEM. SCHOOL
1000 S. Main Street
Baltimore, OH 43105

McKINLEY ELEMENTARY SCHOOL
620 Lynn Street
Findaly, OH 45840

MEDWAY ELEMENTARY SCHOOL
116 Middle Street
Medway, OH 45341

NEW CARLISLE-BETHEL LOCAL SCHOOLS
9760 W. National Road
New Carlisle, OH 45344

NORTH ELEMENTARY SCHOOL
Westgate Drive
Galion, OH 44833

OAKWOOD JR. HIGH SCHOOL
1200 Far Hills Avenue
Dayton, OH 45419

ROOSEVELT ELEMENTARY SCHOOL
1608 W. S sprint Street
Lima, OH 45805

ST. PETER'S ELEMENTARY SCHOOL
63 S. Mulberry Street
Mansfield, Ohio 44902

SHAKER HEIGHTS HIGH SCHOOL
15911 Aldersyde Drive
Shaker Heights, OH 44120

SHREVE ELEMENTARY SCHOOL
598 N. Market Street
Shreve, OH 44676

SPRINGFIELD ARTS COUNCIL
P.O. Box 745
Springfield, OH 45501

STRANAHAN ELEMENTARY SCHOOL
3840 Holland-Sylvania Road
Toledo, OH 43615

TALLMADGE ELEMENTARY SCHOOL
611 Lewis Avenue
Lancaster, OH 43130

VINTON COUNTY HIGH SCHOOL
High Street
McArthur, OH 45651

APPLE CREEK ELEMENTARY SCHOOL
Box 208
Apple Creek, OH 44606

BLUFFTON HIGH SCHOOL
106 W. College Avenue
Bluffton, OH 45817

CLAY HIGH SCHOOL
Route #6
Portsmouth, OH 45662

CLOVERLEAF JR. HIGH SCHOOL
7500 Buffham Road
Seville, OH 44273

DONNELL JR. HIGH SCHOOL
301 Baldwin Avenue
Findlay, OH 45840

DONNELSVILLE ELEMENTARY SCHOOL
150 E. Main Street
Donnelsville, OH 45319

EDISON ELEMENTARY SCHOOL
333 E. Vine Street
Lima, OH 45804

EMERSON ELEMENTARY SCHOOL
650 E. Edwards Street
Lima, OH 45801-3799

FAUROT ELEMENTARY SCHOOL
515 W. Elm Street
Lima, OH 45801

GALLIA COUNTY LOCAL SCHOOLS
220 Jackson Pike
Gallipolis, OH 45631

GALLIPOLIS CITY SCHOOL DISTRICT
463 Second Avenue
Gallipolis, OH 45631

GLENWOOD JR. HIGH SCHOOL
1715 N. Main Street
Findlay, OH 45840

INDIAN VALLEY SCHOOL
510 Enon-Xenia Road
Enon, OH 45323

IRVING ELEMENTARY SCHOOL
1125 N. Metcalf Street
Lima, OH 45801

LIBERTY UNION-THURSTON ELEM. SCHOOL
1000 S. Main Street
Baltimore, OH 43105

MAPLEWOOD ELEMENTARY SCHOOL
1670 Wonderlick Road
Lima, Ohio 45805

MORTON JR. HIGH SCHOOL
231 W. National Road
Vandalia, OH 45377

NEW CARLISLE-BETHEL LOCAL SCHOOL
9760 W. National Road
New Carlisle, OH 45344

NORTHMONT CITY SCHOOLS
4001 Old Salem Road
Englewood, OH 45322

NORTHWEST LOCAL SCHOOLS
8590 Erie Avenue
Canal Fulton, OH 44614

OTTAWA-GLANDORF LOCAL SCHOOLS
630 Glendale Avenue
Ottawa, OH 45875

PARK LAYNE ELEMENTARY SCHOOL
620 Cliffside Drive
New Carlisle, OH 45344

ROOSEVELT ELEMENTARY SCHOOL
1608 W. Spring Street
Lima, OH 45805

ROOSEVELT ELEMENTARY SCHOOL
1409 Coles Blvd.
Portsmouth, OH 45662

ST. MICHAEL SCHOOL
701 Adams Street
Findlay, OH 45840

SEABORN ELEMENTARY SCHOOL
3800 Niles-Carver Road
Mineral Ridge, OH 44440

SEVILLE ELEMENTARY SCHOOL
24 E. Main Street
Seville, OH 44273

SHILOH SCHOOL
Mechanics Street
Shiloh, OH 44878

SMITH JR. HIGH SCHOOL
3625 Little York Road
Dayton, OH 45414

SUMMIT ELEMENTARY SCHOOL
8400 Northport Drive
Cincinnati, OH 45230

TIFFIN ARTS COUNCIL
P.O. Box 684
Tiffin, OH 44883

TUSCARAWAS COUNTY BRD. OF EDUCATION
261 W. High Avenue
New Philadelphia, OH 44663

WESTFIELD ELEMENTARY SCHOOL
9055 S. LeRoy Road
Westfield Center, OH 44251

WHITTIER ELEMENTARY SCHOOL
733 Wyandot Street
Findlay, OH 45840

WHITTIER ELEMENTARY SCHOOL
400 E. Holmes Avenue
Lima, OH 45804